# Media for Health
# Planning, Programmes and Practice

**About the Editor**

**Binod C. Agrawal** is currently the Vice Chancellor of Himgiri Nabh Vishwavidyalaya, Dehradun, Uttarakhand and Director General of TALEEM Research Foundation, Ahmedabad. Earlier, he was associated with ISRO for over two decades where he pioneered the use of qualitative methods for communications research during Satellite Instructional Television Experiment (SITE). Also, he was the founder Director of Mudra Institute of Communications, Ahmedabad.

Dr. Agrawal has over a dozen books to his credit, the most recent being *Ethnography of Communication* (2003) and *Television in South Asia* (2006). Also, he has published over fifty technical and research papers in national and international journals of repute.

# Media for Health

## Planning, Programmes and Practice

*Edited by*
**Binod C. Agrawal**

CONCEPT PUBLISHING COMPANY, NEW DELHI-110 059

**ISBN 13: 978-81-8069-610-7** **ISBN 10: 81-8069-610-3**

First Published 2009

*Published and Printed by*

Concept
Since 1974

**Concept Publishing Company**

**Regd. Office:**

A/15-16, Commercial Block, Mohan Garden
New Delhi-110059 (India)
*Phones* : 25351460, 25351794, *Fax* : 091-11-25357109
*Email* : publishing@conceptpub.com,
website: www.conceptpub.com

**Editorial Office:**

H-13, Bali Nagar, New Delhi-110 015, India.

Cataloging in Publication Data--*Courtesy:* D.K. Agencies (P) Ltd. <docinfo@dkagencies.com>

**Media for health**: planning, programmes and practice/ edited by Binod C. Agrawal.
p. cm.

Contributed articles.
Includes bibliographical references and index..
ISBN 13: 9788180696107 ISBN 10: 8180696103

1. Mass media in health education--India. 2. Communication in public health--India. 3. AIDS (Disease) in mass media. 4. Medical policy--India. 5. India--Scheduled tribes--Health and hygiene. 6. Women's health services--India. I. Agrawal, Binod C. (Binod Chand), 1942-

DDC 362.10954 22

# Introduction

TALEEM Research Foundation (TRF) was established in November 1995 and was registered in May 1996. Since then, the foundation has conducted a variety of research studies. However, two major areas of focus have been healthcare and media effects.

Some issues facing the public health system in India are: controlling HIV/AIDS, improving the health status of women and children, and reducing child morbidity and mortality rates. There is a considerable need to providing appropriate and accessible health services to the entire population and educating the masses on various health issues. Efforts in the areas of public healthcare include the launching and implementation of national-level government programmes such as the National AIDS Control Programme, Child Survival and Safe Motherhood (CSSM) Programme, and Reproductive and Child Health (RCH) Programme.

In this volume, an effort has been made to present some of the research findings based on the studies carried out by the Foundation faculty. Selected studies in the areas of health care and media effects carried out over a period of time.

In the first paper, Dr. Agrawal and Dr. Khan present a comparative analysis of Mass media exposure and awareness of HIV/AIDS and RTI/STI among the Scheduled Tribes of Chhattisgarh and Nagaland. The major hypothesis is that other things being equal regardless of ecological uniqueness and the physical isolation of the Scheduled Tribes, there is no difference between HIV/AIDS awareness among them due to mass media exposure. This paper is based on "Reproductive and Child Health Project, Rapid Household Survey—1998-1999", and is supplemented by existing literature available on various research studies.

Dr. Agrawal, Dr. Kalyan Brata Saha and Dr. Khan in the second paper throw some light on the level of awareness of HIV/AIDS among the Scheduled Castes and Scheduled Tribes women of Assam, Meghalaya and Nagaland. The paper also suggests a communication strategy for the control of HIV/AIDS in the North Eastern region. The data for this paper have been drawn from a large, scale Rapid Household Survey carried out for Reproductive and Child Health (RCH) project, in selected districts of Assam, Meghalaya and Nagaland in 1998.

Dr. Arbind Sinha in paper three discusses health communication needs of the people of Madhya Pradesh and, the functioning IEC in the state. It recommends certain steps to strengthen IEC programme in Madhya Pradesh in order to achieve the goal of "Health for All".

Dr. Chakrabarty and Dr. Patel intend to assess the impact of social marketing on the usage of condoms for reducing the spread of HIV/AIDS in paper four. DKT, a social marketing organization has implemented condom promotion programme in the high-risk areas of Gujarat for preventing HIV/AIDS. The effectiveness of condom for the prevention of HIV/AIDS has been the subject of research for over a decade. Condom social marketing has raised the use of condom in some countries.

In paper five of section two, Dr. Irfan Khan critically examines the issues of health communication and services that are being rendered at grassroots level in Madhya Pradesh. Issues covered include the degree of awareness of Government Health Facilities, perceived sources of information frequency of home visit of health workers and the visit of beneficiaries to Government health centres. This paper is based on primary data in order to assess the health communication needs of health seekers in Madhya Pradesh; secondary data of National Family Health Survey-2 (NFHS-2) and RCM reports. The paper suggests certain measures for effective implementation of Madhya Pradesh Population Policy, 2000.

In paper six, Dr. Khan and Dr. Agrawal attempt to analyze the perception of people about the existing government Health facilities, service providers and the level of patients' satisfaction in the State of Maharashtra. The paper is based on the analyses of data collected in the three Maharashtra Health Surveys: Reproductive and Child Health Project—Rapid Household Survey-2002, Facility Survey under Reproductive and Child Health Project-1999, and Satisfaction Assessment of Patients and Health Providers, 2002. The paper provides some insights into the overall quality of Health services in Maharashtra and draws attention towards areas of concern related to the quality of services.

Dr. Khan and Dr. Chakrabarty in paper seven broadly cover the issues of antenatal, natal and postnatal care, and also propose to compare Madhya Pradesh with other states on achievements related to safe motherhood initiatives.

In paper eight, Dr. Khan and Dr. Verma examine the trend of contraceptive acceptance in India and critically oversea the dynamics between cultural factors and population stabilization programme. The paper is based on secondary data obtained from various Government Documents, and District and National Level Surveys.

Dr. Chakrabarty in paper nine investigates the effect of higher status of the Jaintia women on fertility. It is based on data collected from areas inhabited by the Jaintias, a matriarchal society in the state of Meghalaya, in India.

In paper ten, Dr. Sanon and Dr. Patel examine the perception and interpretation of punishment and its subsequent effects on children, taking into consideration the cultural setting of Rapar taluka, Kutch district of Gujarat. Recommendations are given for the reduction of corporal punishment and the creation of positive attitude about studies in children.

The study of traditional healers assumes great significance in India, especially in tribal dominated states where there seems to have a significant knowledge and understanding gap between the health providers and health seekers, especially among the Scheduled Tribes population. The research study by Dr. Singh and Dr. Agrawal in paper eleven of section four was conducted in four districts of Chhattisgarh with the objective of understanding and identifying the role of healers towards community health and find out how healers perceived and contributed towards the modern health system. The study is expected to provide research inputs for evolving health communication strategy for the state of Chhattisgarh.

This book presents recent studies and findings in the areas of HIV/AIDS related issues; government health services; population stabilization; corporal punishment, and tribal health. Papers in this book are attempts at analyzing various aspects of public health and health communication. The application of media for publicizing health information enables the public to receive information on various issues concerning health and about the availability of different healthcare facilities.

**Binod C. Agrawal**

# Acknowledgements

In the preparation of this book, I received enormous help from individual and the institutions. It is appropriate to record their contribution in preparing the book. I am grateful to International Institute for Population Sciences, Mumbai who gave us the opportunity to carryout "Reproductive and Child Health Project, Rapid Household Survey—1998-99" and "National Family Health Survey (NFHS)" and also Government of India and several international agencies.

I am thankful to all the contributors, namely, Md. Irfan Khan, K.K. Verma, Chandragupt Sanon, Arvind Sinha, Mitali Chakrabarty, Dalip Singh Bora, Kh. Narendra Singh, Dhanji B. Patel and Kalyan Brata Saha. Each of them helped writing the papers to give the present shape of the book. Special thanks go to Michael Vimal Pillai for his careful reading of the book and copy editing of the manuscript. I am grateful to Vijay Uttekar and T.K. Ravindran for their technical support. I am thankful to Ruchi Shukla for her assistance in editing the text. Last but not the least I am grateful to Ashok Mittal and Nitin Mittal of Concept Publishing Company for publishing this book.

**Binod C. Agrawal**
*Editor*

# Contents

## Section Three

## Population, Tribal Health and Corporal Punishment



## Section Four

## Tribal Health, Beliefs and Behavioural Pattern

# List of Tables

# List of Figures

# List of Contributors

**Arvind Sinha**, Ph.D (Sociology, Vikram University, Ujjain), is Professor, Development Communications, Mudra Institute of Communications, Ahmedabad (MICA). He worked as Communication Advisor to the Danish Embassy in India and is on the technical committees of international organizations. Formerly he was Professor, TALEEM Research Foundation and Scientist at Space Application Centre-ISRO, Ahmedabad. He was associated with national and international projects on health and disaster communication and science-society-technology. He has published and co-edited number of books. Professor Sinha has contributed over dozen papers in national and international books and journals. He is referee for three international journals and two major publishing houses in India.

**Binod C. Agrawal,** Ph.D. (Anthropology, University of Wisconsin, Madison, USA), is the Director General, TALEEM Research Foundation, Ahmedabad and Vice Chancellor of Himgiri Nabh Vishwavidyalaya, Dehradun. He is an international communication expert. He was project leader for Satellite Instructional Television Experiment (SITE) social evaluation. He has published over a dozen books and several technical research articles in the national and international journals of social sciences, media and communication.

**Chandragupt Sanon,** Ph.D. (Social Work, Gujarat University, Ahmedabad), is Professor, TALEEM Research Foundation. Formerly, he was Professor and Dean, Faculty of Social Work, Gujarat Vidyapeeth, Ahmedabad having over three decades of teaching and research experience. He published two books and number of research papers in journals. He has been directing and organizing various capacity building programmes for development functionaries.

**Dalip Singh Bora**, Ph.D. (Economics, Kumaun University, Nainital), is Associate Professor in TALEEM Research Foundation. Formerly he was Deputy Registrar, Himgiri Nabh Vishwavidyalaya, Dehradun (Uttarakhand State). He has worked on several projects related to Health and developing Information, Education and Communication (IEC) strategies for health, besides monitoring and evaluation of programmes.

**Dhanji B. Patel,** Ph.D. (Anthropology, Gujarat Vidyapeeth, Ahmedabad). He is Lecturer, TALEEM Research Foundation. He has worked on several social research projects in the field of Health, Community Needs Assessment and developing IEC strategies and media studies.

**Kalyan Brata Saha,** Ph.D. (International Institute for Population Sciences (IIPS), Mumbai) is currently Scientist in ICMR, Jabalpur. Formerly he worked as Research Officer at IIPS, Mumbai and as Research Associate in TALEEM Research Foundation. He is a demographer and his research interest focus on tribal demography, fertility and reproductive health.

**Kh. Narendra Singh,** Ph.D. (Anthropology, University of Pune), is currently working as Senior Consultant, Social Research Institute, New Delhi. He was formerly Associate Professor, TALEEM Research Foundation. His research interest focuses on Nutrition, Reproductive and Child Health, Community Health and Community Needs Assessment Studies.

**Krishna Kumar Verma,** Ph.D. (Anthropology, Ranchi University, Ranchi), is currently Professor, TALEEM Research Foundation. Formerly he was Professor and Head, Anthropology and Sociology, Division, A.N. Sinha Institute of Social Studies, Patna. He has been associated with national and inter-national research projects in demography, communication, women, tribal and development studies. He has published ten books and large number of research papers.

**Md. Irfan Khan** took his Ph.D. degree in Demography from Indian Institute of Technology (IIT), Kanpur. He is currently Professor and Head (Research) in TALEEM Research Foundation, Ahmedabad. He has extensive experience in large scale Population, Health and Social Development studies and has been responsible for undertaking national level surveys like NFHS and DLHS (RCH) in India. His areas of research and development programme evaluation over the past two decades include Fertility and Family Planning, Maternal and Child Health issues, HIV/AIDS, Education, Women Empowerment, Domestic Violence and Social Development.

**Mitali Chakrabarty,** Ph.D. (Anthropology, Gauhati University, Guwahati), is Associate Professor in TALEEM Research Foundation. Formerly she was Social Scientist, National Institute of Nutrition, Hyderabad. She has been extensively involved in large scale national level reproductive and child health studies. She has worked on several evaluation and developmental research related to tobacco exposure, social marketing impact on condom promotion, HIV/AIDS, nutrition and on tribes.

*SECTION ONE*

# HIV/AIDS and Communication Strategies

# 1

# Media, Reproductive Health and Combating HIV/AIDS among Scheduled Tribes of Chhattisgarh and Nagaland

## A Comparative Analysis

*Binod C. Agrawal* and *Md. Irfan Khan*

## Introduction

The HIV/AIDS Pandemic, in the absence of any preventive or curative health care, relies exclusively on protective methods, for which communication in every form, whether electronic or interpersonal are being aggressively employed. HIV/AIDS today has touched the core of the social fabric of a large part of the world. It has affected family, human rights, employment, security, state and family economy like no other Pandemic known to human kind. It is no more confined to certain high-risk behaviour groups like commercial sex-workers or injected drug users. The HIV infection has now largely penetrated various sections of society. Recent HIV/AIDS mapping carried out in various States of India by AIDS control organizations have reported that only few locations were left untouched by HIV/AIDS infection. Geographical trends and epidemiological studies indicate that the infection is being more widespread than it is believed, in the absence of major checks.

In India, the Scheduled Tribes are equally, if not more, susceptible and exposed to HIV/AIDS infection than others. While there are three major ways of the spread of HIV, namely (i) Sexual contact, (ii) Blood transfusion, blood products and stained needles and syringes, and (iii) Vertical transmission—through mother to foetus. The principal mode of transmission in India is primarily heterosexual intercourse with multiple partners and homosexual practice, namely, 'men having sex with men (MSM)'. Furthermore, there is growing evidence that presence of a Sexually Transmitted Disease (STD) greatly facilitates acquisition and transmission of HIV infection, both conditions, by and large associated with the same risk behaviours.

Information and education are the two critical inputs that would help reduce the incidence of HIV/AIDS infection. So the National AIDS Control Programme in India has been trying to inform and educate every section of society about HIV/AIDS preventive methods. For this purpose, in each State, State AIDS Control Societies have been formed, who have evolved area-specific communication strategies to control HIV/AIDS spread in the State. How much and how far they are able to communicate to the people need to be examined in detail for developing better future communication strategy.

The impact of mass media to disseminate the norm of small family seems to be limited in the past and continues to be so "despite massive use of mass media to disseminate the norm of small family, the profile of acceptors has not changed during 1977-90". (Anonymous, 1998: 164). Similar references can be found in several other studies across the world.

Ecological model developed by Stokols (1996) is a framework, a set of theoretical principles for understanding the inter-relationships between diverse personal and environmental multicultural factors in human health and illness at macro-level (Kar, Alkalay and Alex, 2001: 112). Assuming that Chhattisgarh and Nagaland represent two multi-cultural ecologies, a number of factors like interpersonal and community relationships influence health and illness, including HIV/AIDS, which is in turn influenced by media. Since the State and National Health Programmes that affect individual health in both states are common with respect to HIV/AIDS protection their effects would be similar—both in content and nature.

The ecological model enables programmes to understand the complexity of the factors influencing health behaviours and to target these factors at three different levels: Individual, interpersonal and community. Hence, from the ecological perspective, multi-ethnic media campaigns must engage individuals and their environments (Kar, Alkalay and Alex, 2001: 112-13). Within this framework, the paper aims to present a comparative analysis of HIV/AIDS and RTI/STI awareness among the Scheduled Tribes of Chhattisgarh and Nagaland.

## Aim

The aim of this paper is to present a comparative analysis of mass media exposure and awareness of HIV/AIDS and RTI/STI among the Scheduled Tribes of Chhattisgarh and Nagaland. The major hypothesis is that other things being equal, regardless of ecological uniqueness and the physical isolation of the Scheduled Tribes, there are no differences between HIV/AIDS awareness among them due to uniform mass media exposure. Variables taken into consideration for analysis relates to religion, standard of living index, education and media ownership.

This paper is based on "Reproductive and Child Health Project, Rapid Household Survey—1998-1999". It is supplemented by existing literature available on various research studies.

## Data Base

The Reproductive and Child Health Project District Level Survey conducted in the year 2002 in the States of Chhattisgarh and Nagaland form the data base of the paper. It covered 50 per cent of the districts of each State. This way eight districts of Chhattisgarh and four districts of Nagaland are included in the analysis[1].

The main aim of the RCH survey was to collect district level information on reproductive and child healthcare indicators in order to strengthen decentralized planning and implementation of the programme. Since the aim of the paper is to compare media and HIV/AIDS, RTI and STI awareness among the Scheduled Tribes of Chhattisgarh and Nagaland, the Scheduled Tribes were segregated from the total survey. The total currently married women and their husbands interviewed in the survey and the Scheduled Tribes is given in Table 1.1.

**Table 1.1:** Percentage of Scheduled Tribes in the RCH Survey of Chhattisgarh and Nagaland

| *Interviews* | *Chhattisgarh* | *Percentage* | *Nagaland* | *Percentage* |
|---|---|---|---|---|
| Total married women | 6278 | 100.0 | 2813 | 100.0 |
| Total Scheduled Tribes married women | 1814 | 28.9 | 2680 | 95.3 |
| Total married men (husband) interviewed | 4670 | 100.0 | 2716 | 100.0 |
| Total Scheduled Tribes married men (husband) | 1414 | 30.3 | 2583 | 95.1 |

The analysis included eligible women in the age group of 15-45 and men (husbands), who were in most cases older than their wives. Table 1.1 shows the analysis covered 1814 (28.9 per cent) women and 1414 (30.3 per cent) men in Chhattisgarh and 2680 (95.3 per cent) women and 2583 (95.1 per cent) men in Nagaland. The percentage of Scheduled Tribes in the Table sample is comparable to those of the population of these two States.

## Tribes of Chhattisgarh and Nagaland

The States of Chhattisgarh and Nagaland were carved out from the States of Madhya Pradesh and Assam and North-Eastern Frontier Agency in the year 2001 and 1963 respectively. The basis of separation was the distinct tribal and cultural identities of these two States. In this respect, both states have distinct tribal characteristics and continue to live in somewhat isolated condition and have limited economic resources.

Chhattisgarh is in the central part of the country and has a total population of about 20.7 million (20,795,956; according to Census of India, 2001) in a geographical area of 135,191 sq. km. and is the ninth largest State of the country. Chhattisgarh has 31.76 per cent Scheduled Tribe population. The tribal population are concentrated in the remote and densely forested Northern and Southern regions. Dantewada district has the highest (79 per cent) Scheduled Tribe population, whereas the lowest is in Mahasamund (28 per cent). Gond—the largest of the Scheduled Tribes, are spread throughout the State and on the adjoining States so are the several other tribes. The Scheduled Tribes of Chhattisgarh are diverse in location, origin, socio-cultural history, language, means of livelihood and level of development. The Northern region of the State is the home of Oraons, Kawar, Majhi, Bharia, Agaria, Nagasia, Khairwar, Dhanwar and Korwas. The Southern region comprising of Bastar and Dantewada districts have very high tribal concentration and are populated by various tribes such as Gond, Bhatra, Halba, Maria and Pardhi.

Nagaland, on the other hand is one of the country's smallest States having less than 2 million population (1,988,636 according to Census of India, 2001) having one of the highest population growth in the country (64.41 per cent growth between 1991-2001). Nagaland is situated in the extreme north-east region of the country touching the international border with Myanmar. Though Nagaland is largely a tribal state of Christian faith, it constitutes a number of tribes who speak different languages, viz. Ao, Chang, Chakesang, Sanglam, Konyak, Angami, Sema and Lotha. In spite of linguistic diversity common religion of Christianity adopted little over a century ago contributed to the development of Naga identity. "This was the creation of ecclesiastical structures. When members of a tribe become Christian they were organized into local Churches, when these local Churches were numerous enough they were first to bring together the representatives of the whole tribe which they went a long way to strengthen the tribal identity" (Nag, 2002: 146).

In case of Chhattisgarh, no such tribal identity can be found. On the contrary, the cultural diversity is visible throughout the State. Chhattisgarh has some of the primitive tribes like Kamar, Abhujmaria, Hill Korwa, Birhor and Baiga. The cultural diversity shows a very weak inter-tribal interaction and communication. On the other hand, in Nagaland one observes a high degree of inter-tribal interaction having direct communication implications in promoting HIV/AIDS awareness. The comparative analysis of the HIV/AIDS awareness must be viewed within this perspective.

## Analysis

### *Comparative Socio-economic Profile*

The respondents of the study consisted of married women in the age group of 15-44 and their husbands (men), who were slightly older than women. This is clearly reflected in the age distribution of the respondents in which there are more women in the younger age groups as compared to men (*See* Table 1.2). In this respect, all respondents could be considered as adults in the sexually active age group, who were most vulnerable to HIV/AIDS, RTI and STI infection through various modes of transmission, especially in case of unprotected sexual encounters (*See* Table 1.2).

The contrasting characteristics highlighted in the analysis are the religious background of the respondents where most Chhattisgarh respondents belonged to the Hindu religion as opposed to the Nagaland respondents, almost exclusively Christian (*See* Table 1.2).

Table 1.2 shows high literacy rate among men as opposed to women in both States, though on the whole, the literacy rates are much lower in Chhattisgarh as compared to Nagaland. (Chhattisgarh 38.6 per cent and Nagaland 80.8 per cent). The Standard of Living Index was developed to measure the economic status of the household.[2] The Standard of Living Index (SLI) shows that more than 87 per cent Chhattisgarh tribes belonged to low standard of living, which is near or below poverty line in the State as compared to little over 55.6 per cent in the same category in Nagaland (Table 1.2).

Further, an analysis was attempted from the total survey to compute the overall ownership of radio and television. Table 1.3 shows that Chhattisgarh lagged far behind (Radio 15.1 per cent and TV 11.7 per cent) as compared to Nagaland (Radio

43.4 per cent, TV 35 per cent), thereby reflecting higher degree of electronic media access in Nagaland as compared to Chhattisgarh.

**Table 1.2:** Socio-economic and Educational Background

| *Background Characteristics* | *Chhattisgarh* | | | *Nagaland* | | |
|---|---|---|---|---|---|---|
| | *Women* | *Men* | *Total* | *Women* | *Men* | *Total* |
| **Age** | | | | | | |
| Less than 20 years | 6.2 | 3.5 | 5.0 | 1.9 | 0.3 | 1.1 |
| 20-34 years | 68.5 | 46.9 | 59.0 | 53.1 | 28.5 | 41.0 |
| 35 years and above | 25.3 | 49.6 | 36.0 | 45.0 | 71.2 | 57.9 |
| **Education** | | | | | | |
| Literate | 23.6 | 57.9 | 38.6 | 77.1 | 84.7 | 80.8 |
| Non-literate | 76.4 | 42.1 | 61.4 | 22.9 | 15.3 | 19.2 |
| **Religion** | | | | | | |
| Hindu | 99.3 | 99.6 | 99.4 | 0.2 | 0.2 | 0.4 |
| Non-Hindu | 0.7 | 0.4 | 0.6 | 99.8 | 99.8 | 99.6 |
| **Standard of Living Index** | | | | | | |
| Low | 86.9 | 87.5 | 87.2 | 51.5 | 51.6 | 51.5 |
| Medium | 10.3 | 9.7 | 10.0 | 35.5 | 35.2 | 35.4 |
| High | 2.8 | 2.8 | 2.8 | 13.0 | 13.2 | 13.1 |
| **Total** | **1814** | **1414** | **2228** | **2680** | **2583** | **5263** |

The analysis of socio-economic and educational characteristics indicates clear differences between Chhattisgarh and Nagaland Scheduled Tribes.

### Awareness of HIV/AIDS

On the whole, there is a relative low level of awareness of HIV/AIDS and RTI/STI among the Chhattisgarh respondents as compared to Nagaland (Table 1.3). Though the awareness is higher among men as compared to women, these differences are statistically insignificant in case of Nagaland as compared to Chhattisgarh. It is important to point-out that four out of five men and women in Nagaland are aware of HIV/AIDS, which could be amongst the highest in the country as a whole (82.0 per cent women and 85.3 per cent men). In this respect,

Chhattisgarh Scheduled Tribes are far behind in awareness level of HIV/AIDS. It is not surprising to note that RTI/STI awareness level is also below 50 per cent in both states, though Chhattisgarh lags behind in absolute numbers (Table 1.3). It may be concluded that HIV/AIDS awareness is higher in the north-eastern region as compared to the tribes of central Indian region. This would be equally true for the general population in these two regions.

**Table 1.3:** Awareness of HIV/AIDS and RTI/STI

| *Awareness Level* | *Chhattisgarh* | *Nagaland* |
|---|---|---|
| **Awareness of HIV/AIDS** | | |
| Women | 9.3 | 82.0 |
| Men | 28.3 | 85.3 |
| **Total** | **17.6** | **83.6** |
| **Awareness of RTI/STI** | | |
| Women | 5.3 | 43.0 |
| Men | 12.4 | 48.8 |
| **Total** | **8.4** | **45.8** |

The ecological model for the multi-cultural communication framework clearly indicates that at the environmental level, the degree of isolation of the Scheduled Tribes had in noway influenced the degree of awareness of HIV/AIDS as seen in Nagaland, compared to Chhattisgarh. Therefore, it would be important to examine this point at the individual and community level factors like education and household Standard of Living Index (SLI). Further, it would be equally important to examine sources of information of the different mass media and compare the same with the ownership of mass media along with inter-personal communication as reflected in Table 1.4.

**Table 1.4:** Ownership of Radio and Television among Scheduled Tribes

| *Media* | *Chhattisgarh* | *Nagaland* |
|---|---|---|
| Radio | 15.1 | 43.4 |
| Television | 11.7 | 35.0 |
| **Total Number of Households** | 2078 | 4152 |

## Mass Media and HIV/AIDS Awareness

On the whole, the picture of awareness remains somewhat similar as men, more than women, seemed to have been exposed to mass media like radio, television, newspapers and outdoor publicity and have learnt about HIV/AIDS more than women in both States (Table 1.5). However, this percentage is higher among the Scheduled Tribes of Nagaland as compared to Chhattisgarh. Exception is TV where almost three-fourth of the women in Chhattisgarh (74.1 per cent) and 51.9 per cent men claimed to have known about HIV/AIDS through TV as compared to 27 per cent women and 37 per cent men who reported TV as a source of information of HIV/AIDS in Nagaland (Table 1.5).

**Table 1.5:** Mass Media and Awareness of HIV/AIDS

| *Media* | *Chhattisgarh* | | | *Nagaland* | | |
|---|---|---|---|---|---|---|
| | *Women* | *Men* | *Total* | *Women* | *Men* | *Total* |
| Radios | 22.5 | 27.6 | 26.1 | 30.6 | 49.4 | 39.8 |
| Televisions | 74.1 | 51.9 | 58.5 | 27.0 | 37.0 | 31.8 |
| Newspapers/ Books/Magazines | 13.0 | 23.2 | 20.2 | 33.6 | 50.6 | 41.9 |
| Slogans/Pamphlets/ Posters/Wall Hoardings | 6.9 | 21.8 | 17.4 | 26.6 | 35.8 | 31.0 |
| **Total** | **169** | **401** | **570** | **2196** | **2203** | **4399** |

It is difficult to explain this contrast in findings, especially when there are more respondents having TV access in Nagaland as compared to Chhattisgarh. [TV ownership 11.7 per cent in Chhattisgarh and 35 per cent in Nagaland (Table 1.3)]. Authors have observed in earlier studies that there was a high degree of video viewership in Nagaland in mid-eighties. It was because Doordarshan carried mostly Hindi programmes. After 1992, viewing of English channels, especially MTV, Channel V and other transnational channels became popular in Nagaland. Nagaland viewers, in spite of regional channels by Doordarshan, continued to view transnational channels. This may explain why TV viewers of Nagaland did not indicate TV as a source of HIV/AIDS, RTI/STI information, since TV channels, especially transnational channels don't carry such health messages (Agrawal *et al.*, 1989).

In case of print media and outdoor publicity, the picture about HIV/AIDS awareness was similar to that of radio and TV for both States. It would not be out of place to mention that mass media as a whole was a major source of HIV/AIDS awareness in Nagaland as compared to Chhattisgarh. The same holds true for the awareness of RTI/STI (Table 1.6).

**Table 1.6:** Mass Media and Awareness of RTI/STI

| *Media* | *Chhattisgarh* | | | *Nagaland* | | |
|---|---|---|---|---|---|---|
| | *Women* | *Men* | *Total* | *Women* | *Men* | *Total* |
| Radios | 12.2 | 28.9 | 23.0 | 22.8 | 33.1 | 28.2 |
| Televisions | 40.1 | 36.5 | 37.8 | 20.6 | 28.7 | 24.8 |
| Newspapers/ Books/Magazines | 40.1 | 24.8 | 30.2 | 31.1 | 44.6 | 38.2 |
| Slogans/Pamphlets/ Posters/Wall Hoardings | 3.4 | 16.9 | 12.2 | 20.9 | 25.4 | 23.3 |
| **Total** | **95** | **175** | **270** | **1151** | **1262** | **2413** |

## Interpersonal Communication

### *HIV/AIDS Awareness*

The most remarkable finding is that the health-workers have consistently been the source of information of HIV/AIDS for men and women in both States (14.3 per cent in Chhattisgarh and 16.1 per cent in Nagaland—*See* Table 1.7), though it is slightly lower in case of Chhattisgarh women (Table 1.7). Interaction of the health-workers with the people may be the source of information even in the remotest part of the country. On the other hand, school teachers were reported to be least source of information of HIV/AIDS. For the highest percentage of people, the source of HIV/AIDS information remained friends and relatives, though it is manifold higher in Nagaland as compared to Chhattisgarh (Table 1.7). This is because of the strong and coherent social organization in Nagaland as compared to Chhattisgarh, where lack of tribal identity and education does not permit inter-tribal communication, as explained in the ecological model.

**Table 1.7:** Interpersonal Communication and Awareness of HIV/AIDS

| *Interpersonal Communication* | *Chhattisgarh* | | | *Nagaland* | | |
|---|---|---|---|---|---|---|
| | *Women* | *Men* | *Total* | *Women* | *Men* | *Total* |
| Doctor | 3.2 | 13.9 | 10.7 | 22.6 | 26.3 | 24.3 |
| Health-Worker | 10.9 | 15.7 | 14.3 | 15.9 | 16.5 | 16.1 |
| School Teacher | 0.0 | 0.2 | 0.1 | 5.7 | 5.6 | 5.6 |
| Community Meetings | 5.1 | 5.9 | 5.7 | 18.4 | 19.4 | 18.8 |
| Friends/Relations | 17.9 | 27.7 | 24.8 | 62.9 | 58.1 | 60.1 |
| **Total** | **169** | **401** | **570** | **2196** | **2203** | **4399** |

The pattern is in noway different in the case of RTI/STI, though the percentage of the awareness of RTI/STI is somewhat higher as compared to HIV/AIDS in Chhattisgarh and in Nagaland in few categories (Table 1.8).

**Table 1.8:** Interpersonal Communication and Awareness of RTI/STI

| *Interpersonal Communication* | *Chhattisgarh* | | | *Nagaland* | | |
|---|---|---|---|---|---|---|
| | *Women* | *Men* | *Total* | *Women* | *Men* | *Total* |
| Doctor | 5.2 | 12.1 | 9.7 | 18.9 | 23.4 | 21.3 |
| Health-Worker | 12.1 | 17.2 | 15.4 | 13.9 | 16.2 | 15.1 |
| School Teacher | 0.0 | 0.5 | 0.3 | 5.7 | 6.9 | 6.3 |
| Community Meetings | 5.4 | 5.1 | 5.2 | 16.2 | 14.3 | 15.2 |
| Friends/Relation | 38.7 | 30.8 | 33.6 | 67.6 | 62.1 | 64.7 |
| **Total** | **95** | **175** | **270** | **1151** | **1262** | **2413** |

Further analysis indicated that the high degree of literacy, higher standard of living index and religion among Nagaland Scheduled Tribes as compared to Chhattisgarh Scheduled Tribes might explain the variations in the degree of HIV/AIDS and RTI/STI awareness as indicated in Tables 1.9 to 1.12.

**Table 1.9:** Percentages of RTI/STI Awareness by Mass Media, Education, and Standard of Living Index

| *Variable* | *Chhattisgarh* | | | *Nagaland* | | |
|---|---|---|---|---|---|---|
| | *Women* | *Men* | *Total* | *Women* | *Men* | *Total* |
| | *No Exposure to Mass Media* | | | | | |
| **Education** | | | | | | |
| Literate | 34.8 | 70.5 | 54.1 | 71.2 | 82.3 | 76.1 |
| Non-literate | 65.2 | 29.5 | 45.9 | 28.8 | 17.7 | 23.9 |
| **Standard of Living** | | | | | | |
| Low | 80.7 | 86.3 | 83.7 | 61.0 | 63.1 | 61.9 |
| Medium | 15.7 | 9.8 | 12.5 | 30.3 | 28.8 | 29.6 |
| High | 3.6 | 3.9 | 3.8 | 8.7 | 8.2 | 8.5 |
| **Total** | **51** | **60** | **111** | **589** | **468** | **1057** |
| | *Exposure to Mass Media* | | | | | |
| **Education** | | | | | | |
| Literate | 72.7 | 91.6 | 86.3 | 93.7 | 97.4 | 95.9 |
| Non-literate | 27.3 | 8.4 | 13.7 | 6.3 | 2.6 | 4.1 |
| **Standard of Living** | | | | | | |
| Low | 32.1 | 57.8 | 50.5 | 27.7 | 31.7 | 30.0 |
| Medium | 37.8 | 31.8 | 33.5 | 41.3 | 43.5 | 42.6 |
| High | 30.1 | 10.4 | 16.0 | 31.0 | 24.8 | 27.4 |
| **Total** | **45** | **114** | **159** | **562** | **794** | **1356** |

**Table 1.10:** Percentages of RTI/STI Awareness by Interpersonal Communication, Education, and Standard of Living Index

| *Variable* | *Chhattisgarh* | | | *Nagaland* | | |
|---|---|---|---|---|---|---|
| | *Women* | *Men* | *Total* | *Women* | *Men* | *Total* |
| | *No Exposure to Interpersonal Communication* | | | | | |
| **Education** | | | | | | |
| Literate | 81.2 | 88.1 | 85.7 | 95.8 | 97.7 | 96.9 |
| Non-literate | 18.8 | 11.9 | 14.3 | 4.2 | 2.3 | 3.1 |
| **Standard of Living** | | | | | | |
| Low | 38.3 | 50.7 | 46.3 | 23.2 | 26 | 24.9 |
| Medium | 38 | 36.3 | 36.9 | 34.5 | 40.4 | 38.0 |
| High | 23.7 | 13.1 | 16.8 | 42.2 | 33.6 | 37.1 |
| **Total** | **40** | **74** | **114** | **188** | **277** | **465** |
| | *Exposure to Interpersonal Communication* | | | | | |
| **Education** | | | | | | |
| Literate | 32.2 | 81.6 | 64.0 | 79.5 | 90.2 | 84.9 |
| Non-literate | 67.8 | 18.4 | 36.0 | 20.5 | 9.8 | 15.1 |
| **Standard of Living** | | | | | | |
| Low | 71.9 | 80.2 | 77.2 | 48.9 | 48.2 | 48.5 |
| Medium | 17.6 | 15.3 | 16.1 | 35.9 | 37.4 | 36.7 |
| High | 10.5 | 4.6 | 6.7 | 15.2 | 14.4 | 14.8 |
| **Total** | **56** | **101** | **157** | **963** | **985** | **1948** |

**Table 1.11:** Percentages of HIV/AIDS Awareness by Mass Media, Education, and Standard of Living Index

| *Variable* | *Chhattisgarh* | | | *Nagaland* | | |
|---|---|---|---|---|---|---|
| | *Women* | *Men* | *Total* | *Women* | *Men* | *Total* |
| | *No Exposure to Mass Media* | | | | | |
| **Education** | | | | | | |
| Literate | 64.1 | 76.5 | 73.9 | 70.5 | 70.0 | 70.3 |
| Non-literate | 35.9 | 23.5 | 26.1 | 29.5 | 30.0 | 29.7 |
| **Standard of Living** | | | | | | |
| Low | 85.7 | 94.1 | 92.3 | 67.9 | 75.7 | 70.5 |
| Medium | 11.3 | 4.4 | 5.9 | 27.8 | 21.3 | 25.6 |
| High | 3.0 | 1.5 | 1.8 | 4.2 | 3.0 | 3.8 |
| **Total** | **26** | **97** | **123** | **898** | **452** | **1350** |
| | *Exposure to Mass Media* | | | | | |
| **Education** | | | | | | |
| Literate | 72.9 | 92.4 | 86.2 | 92.4 | 94.9 | 93.8 |
| Non-literate | 27.1 | 7.6 | 13.8 | 7.6 | 5.1 | 6.2 |
| **Standard of Living** | | | | | | |
| Low | 33.3 | 59.3 | 51.0 | 32.1 | 40.1 | 36.7 |
| Medium | 48.4 | 30.6 | 36.3 | 45.1 | 41.9 | 43.3 |
| High | 18.3 | 10.1 | 12.7 | 22.9 | 18.0 | 20.1 |
| **Total** | **143** | **304** | **447** | **1298** | **1750** | **3048** |

**Table 1.12:** Percentages of HIV/AIDS Awareness by Interpersonal Communication, Education, Standard of Living Index

| *Variable* | *Chhattisgarh* | | | *Nagaland* | | |
|---|---|---|---|---|---|---|
| | *Women* | *Men* | *Total* | *Women* | *Men* | *Total* |
| | *No Exposure to Interpersonal Communication* | | | | | |
| **Education** | | | | | | |
| Literate | 73.5 | 90.6 | 84.3 | 94.5 | 95.3 | 94.9 |
| Non-literate | 26.5 | 9.4 | 15.7 | 5.5 | 4.7 | 5.1 |
| **Standard of Living** | | | | | | |
| Low | 32.4 | 58.7 | 49.0 | 32.1 | 34.0 | 33.1 |
| Medium | 50.8 | 30.8 | 38.1 | 37.6 | 41.6 | 39.8 |
| High | 16.8 | 10.5 | 12.8 | 30.3 | 24.5 | 27.1 |
| **Total** | **115** | **198** | **313** | **404** | **499** | **903** |
| | *Exposure to Interpersonal Communication* | | | | | |
| **Education** | | | | | | |
| Literate | 67.3 | 86.6 | 82.5 | 81.0 | 88.2 | 84.5 |
| Non-literate | 32.7 | 13.4 | 17.5 | 19.0 | 11.8 | 15.5 |
| **Standard of Living** | | | | | | |
| Low | 61.0 | 76.6 | 73.3 | 50.1 | 51.4 | 50.7 |
| Medium | 25.0 | 17.9 | 19.4 | 38.1 | 36.5 | 37.3 |
| High | 14.1 | 5.5 | 7.3 | 11.8 | 12.1 | 11.9 |
| **Total** | **54** | **203** | **257** | **1793** | **1704** | **3497** |

## Conclusion

The analysis presented so far does not warrant rejection of the hypothesis that regardless of ecological uniqueness and physical isolation there would be no differences about HIV/AIDS and RTI/STI awareness among the Scheduled Tribes of Chhattisgarh and Nagaland due to uniform mass media exposure. It is because of the historical factors, which led to the creation of a single identity among the Scheduled Tribes of Nagaland, as opposed to Chhattisgarh, where nothing of this sort happened even over a period of time. Also, interpersonal communications with friends, relatives and health-workers in both States remain an important source of information of HIV/AIDS and RTI/STI. Further analysis has indicated a dominant role of literacy in acquiring HIV/AIDS and RTI/STI awareness from mass media as well as interpersonal communication. In spite of mass media ownership and availability, individual choices for accessing information source have determined the kind of health information the people would receive. This is the reason why television has not been an important source of HIV/AIDS information in Nagaland as compared to Chhattisgarh.

It is, therefore, recommended that in order to cross over the ecological and literacy barrier, a multipronged campaign would be required in which both mass media and interpersonal communication must be equally emphasized to increase HIV/AIDS and RTI/STI awareness.

### *Acknowledgements*

The authors gratefully acknowledge the valuable assistance of Shri Vijay Uttaker, who carried out the analysis and prepared Power Point presentations and graphics. Also thanks are due to Ms. Shalini Raghaviah for editorial and writing assistance.

## NOTES

1. We are grateful to International Institute for Population Sciences (IIPS), Mumbai which coordinated this national level survey as Nodal Agency and provided us the total data for further analysis. Please refer DLHS-RCH reports of IIPS, Mumbai for more details.
2. The index is based on scores given to the reported household amenities such as source of drinking water, type of house, source of lighting, types of cooking fuel, toilet facility and ownership of items like radio, television, sewing machine, telephone, etc. The total score varies from a minimum of 0 to a maximum of 40. Low SLI classified if the total score falls between 0-9, score 10-19 categorised for medium and scores greater than 19 was categorised for high SLI.

## REFERENCES

Agrawal, Binod C. *et al.* (1989), *Communication Revolution: A Study of Video Penetration in India.* Ahmedabad: DECU, ISRO (Report).

Anonymous (1998), Monitoring and Evaluation of Family Planning Programme. In *Health Management* (Vol. 1); pp. 157-182. New Delhi: National Institute of Health and Family Welfare.

Kar, Snehendu B., Rina Alkalay with Shana Alex (2001), Communicating with Multi-cultural Populations—A Theoretical Framework. In *Health Communication—Multicultural Perspective.* S.B. Kar, R. Alkalay with Shana Alex (eds.); pp. 109-137. New Delhi/London: Sage Publications, Inc.

Nag, Sajal (2002), Naga Identity: Formation, Construction and Expansion. In *Dimensions of Development in Nagaland.* C.S. Thomas and Gurudas Das (eds.); pp. 141-155. New Delhi: Regency Publications.

Stokols, D. (1996), Translating Social Ecological Theory with Guidelines for Community Health Promotion. *American Journal of Health Promotion,* 10 (4), 282-298.

Vaishnav, T.K. (2004), *Scheduled Tribes of Chhattisgarh* (In Hindi). Raipur: Tribal Research and Training Institute.

# 2

# Healthcare Communication for HIV/AIDS Control Among Scheduled Tribes and Scheduled Castes Women in North-Eastern Region of India

*Binod C. Agrawal, Kalyan Brata Saha* and *Md. Irfan Khan*

## Introduction

HIV/AIDS has been seen as the number one enemy of humans in the 21st century. India has become one of the largest victims of HIV/AIDS. HIV/AIDS spread has opened up a Pandora of medical and health problems apart from creating acute socio-psychological trauma for the victims and their families. However an average person in the street seems to be unconcerned and is not willing to discuss the consequences of unprotected sex—one of the major vehicles for the spread of HIV/AIDS. Currently in India, HIV/AIDS is spilling into all sections of society and is more widespread than people are willing to believe. "It has been estimated that if transmission of HIV/AIDS continues at the same pace, about 5 million persons in India would be infected by the year 2000 and the number of AIDS cases would exceed one million" (Anonymous, 2000: 1). As of now, there is no vaccine or cure that would protect human beings against HIV/AIDS. At the same time, few people across the country have correct knowledge and understanding of the mode of transmission of HIV/AIDS, in other words prevention methods.

Education through communication is imperative for the prevention of HIV/AIDS. Despite the national commitment towards communication of HIV/AIDS related messages, not much has been achieved so far. Adequate resources have been allocated, mass awareness campaigns have been organized, distribution of free condoms have been taken up albeit with limited success. A number of STD clinics have also been set up with the hope that they would help in curbing the rapid spread of HIV/AIDS, though little is known about its effects.

The present paper throws some light on the level of awareness of HIV/AIDS among the Scheduled Castes and Scheduled Tribes women of Assam, Meghalaya and Nagaland. The paper also suggests a communication strategy for the control of HIV/AIDS in North-Eastern region.

**Survey**

The data for the paper have been drawn from a large scale Rapid Household Survey carried out for Reproductive and Child Health (RCH) project sponsored by the Ministry of Health and Family Welfare, Government of India in 18 districts covering three States of Assam, Meghalaya and Nagaland[1]. In each of the 18 districts, 1000 households were randomly selected from 50 locations. In each household, Currently Married Women (CMW) in the age group of 15-44 years were interviewed with the help of a "questionnaire" specially designed to assess how women have utilized the healthcare services provided by the Government. The survey was carried out in the second half of 1998. Specially trained investigators locally recruited and trained for this purpose collected the data. The survey covered 12,960 currently married women in Assam, 3,062 in Meghalaya and 3,141 in Nagaland. From the total sample of 19,163 respondents, 8,421 Scheduled Castes and Scheduled Tribes respondents from the three States were separated for the present analysis.

---

1. The World Bank supported study has been sponsored by the Ministry of Health and Family Welfare, Government of India for a period of five years. The author acknowledges the source and is sincerely thankful to the Government for the use of the data for the preparation of this paper [for details see Rapid Household Survey RCH Project Phase I (1998) of Assam, Meghalaya and Nagaland; TALEEM Research Foundation, Ahmedabad (2000)].

## Analysis

The analysis attempts to highlight the current level of information about HIV/AIDS amongst these respondents and check for differences if any, by religion, age and education, the type of house of the women. Analysis also seeks their sources of information about HIV/AIDS, knowledge about the mode of transmission and methods of prevention of HIV/AIDS. The existing misconceptions about HIV/AIDS have been included. Since Meghalaya and Nagaland have predominantly Christian population whereas Assam has Hindu population, a comparison of the responses of Christian and Hindu respondents have been made for evolving broad communication strategy for North-Eastern region.

## Respondents' Characteristics

Scheduled Tribes dominate the sample. Scheduled Castes presence in the sample in all three States put together is little over five per cent. While 64.9 per cent respondents are Christian, 33.0 per cent are Hindu, and the remaining 2.1 per cent belonged to other religions (Table 2.1). One-third or 33.2 per cent respondents are illiterate and the remaining are literate, with education ranging from standard I to X and above.

**Table 2.1:** Women Respondents by Age and Religion

| *Age Groups* | *Religion* | | | *Total* |
|---|---|---|---|---|
| | *Christian* | *Hindu* | *Others ** | |
| 15-19 | 2.1 | 2.0 | 0.6 | 2.0 |
| 20-29 | 42.6 | 38.6 | 41.3 | 41.3 |
| 30-39 | 36.7 | 40.4 | 32.6 | 37.8 |
| 40-44 | 18.7 | 19.0 | 25.6 | 18.9 |
| **Total** | **5469 (64.9)** | **2780 (33.0)** | **172 (2.1)** | **8421 (100.0)** |

* Others include Muslim, Buddhist, Sikh and others.

The literacy rate, it seems, in three States is much above the national female literacy rate, that too among younger age groups (Table 2.2). The analysis reflects an increasing demand of education among Scheduled Castes and Scheduled Tribes in North-Eastern region of the country. Majority of the women live in *kachcha* houses (53.7 per cent) followed by semi-*pucca* houses (37.4 per cent) (Table 2.3). It seems that Assam women reflect 'relative poverty' as compared to Nagaland and Meghalaya.

**Table 2.2:** Women Respondents by Age and Education

| *Age Groups* | *Education* | | | | *Total* |
|---|---|---|---|---|---|
| | *Illiterate* | *Class 1-5* | *Class 6-9* | *Class 10+* | |
| 15-19 | 23.5 | 18.2 | 37.1 | 21.2 | 170 |
| 20-29 | 25.1 | 16.3 | 28.8 | 29.8 | 3474 |
| 30-39 | 33.8 | 17.8 | 25.4 | 23.0 | 3184 |
| 40-44 | 50.8 | 17.6 | 18.8 | 12.8 | 1593 |
| **Total** | **2798 (33.2)** | **1445 (17.2)** | **2171 (25.8)** | **2007 (23.8)** | **8421 (100.0)** |

**Table 2.3:** Percentage Distribution of Women Respondents by House Type and State

| *Type of House* | *States* | | | *Total* |
|---|---|---|---|---|
| | *Assam* | *Meghalaya* | *Nagaland* | |
| *Pucca* | 6.7 | 16.1 | 3.6 | 8.8 |
| Semi-*pucca* | 18.2 | 53.4 | 41.8 | 37.4 |
| *Kachcha* | 75.0 | 30.5 | 54.5 | 53.7 |
| **Total** | **2916** | **2751** | **2754** | **8421** |

## Age at Cohabitation

According to Table 2.4 married women reported an early sexual experience with first cohabitation below or around 15 years (6.6 per cent). However, 46.0 per cent have reported having first sexual experience at 20 years of age (Table 2.4). Differences have been observed among various religious groups in which Hindu women have reported having early cohabitation compared to Christian and other religious groups. These differences may be due to early marriages among the Hindus. It shows sexual experiences and encounter of sex early in their lives. It is, therefore, suggested that HIV/AIDS campaign must be targeted to young girls and women regardless of their religious, tribal or non-tribal background. Since literacy rate is high among these women, it is suggested that educational institutions may be an appropriate starting point for communication.

**Table 2.4:** Women Respondents by Age at Cohabitation and Religion

| *Age at Cohabitation (in years)* | *Religion* | | | *Total* |
|---|---|---|---|---|
| | *Christian* | *Hindu* | *Others ** | |
| Up to 15 | 4.4 | 11.0 | 5.8 | 6.6 |
| 16 | 5.6 | 9.6 | 4.1 | 6.9 |
| 17 | 7.4 | 9.9 | 4.7 | 8.2 |
| 18 | 19.0 | 16.6 | 16.3 | 18.2 |
| 19 | 15.3 | 12.2 | 11.0 | 14.2 |
| 20 | 48.3 | 40.8 | 58.1 | 46.0 |
| **Total** | **5469 (64.9)** | **2780 (33.1)** | **172 (2.0)** | **8421 (100.0)** |

* Others include Muslim, Buddhist, Sikh and others.

## HIV/AIDS Awareness

"Have you heard of any illness called HIV/AIDS"? This question was uniformly asked to all respondents. Table 2.5 shows that on the whole 57.1 per cent women had heard of HIV/AIDS in all the three States. Further Table 2.5 shows that the women in the age group of 20-29 years had heard most about HIV/AIDS (63.0 per cent) and least informed were in 40-44 years age group (48.0 per cent). The HIV/AIDS was no threat and unheard by these women twenty years ago when they were growing. It is not surprising that more urban women in the age group of 20-29 years had heard of HIV/AIDS (89.2 per cent) than their rural counterpart (59.9 per cent), due to high electronic media exposure.

There are sharp differences of HIV/AIDS awareness between illiterate rural and literate urban women (Table 2.5). The rural illiterate women had heard least about HIV/AIDS whereas urban literate women had heard most about it (illiterate rural women 19.7 per cent as opposed to literate urban women 92.2 per cent). Improvement in educational opportunities for rural women may be the key to enhancing any information level including HIV/AIDS.

Broadly, the "Economic Status" of the women has been gauged with the help of their residential accommodation classified as *pucca*, semi-*pucca* and *kachcha*. There seems to be a positive association between degree of HIV/AIDS information and economic status of the respondents. Both rural and urban women living in *pucca* houses knew more about HIV/AIDS (78.8 per cent and 90.4 per cent) as opposed to rural and urban living in *kachcha* house (38.1 per cent and 77.9 per cent) (Table 2.5). A similar pattern can be observed between Hindu and Christian women (Hindu 37.9 per cent and Christian 66.8 per cent).

**Table 2.5:** Percentage Distribution of Respondents Heard of HIV/AIDS by Age, Education, House Type, Religion and Residential Location

| | *Heard* | | | *Not Heard* | | |
|---|---|---|---|---|---|---|
| | *Rural* | *Urban* | *Total* | *Rural* | *Urban* | *Total* |
| *Age* | | | | | | |
| 15-19 | 49.7 | 61.5 | 50.6 | 50.3 | 38.5 | 49.4 |
| 20-29 | 59.9 | 89.2 | 63.0 | 40.1 | 10.8 | 37.0 |
| 30-39 | 50.7 | 88.8 | 55.6 | 49.3 | 11.2 | 44.4 |
| 40-44 | 43.5 | 82.4 | 48.0 | 56.5 | 17.6 | 52.0 |
| *Education* | | | | | | |
| Illiterate | 19.7 | 55.2 | 21.5 | 80.3 | 44.8 | 78.5 |
| 1-5 Class | 54.7 | 78.8 | 55.3 | 45.3 | 21.2 | 44.7 |
| 6-9 Class | 72.6 | 86.6 | 74.1 | 27.4 | 13.4 | 25.9 |
| 10+ Class | 87.2 | 96.0 | 89.7 | 12.8 | 4.0 | 10.3 |
| *Type of House* | | | | | | |
| *Pucca* | 78.8 | 90.4 | 82.2 | 21.2 | 9.6 | 17.8 |
| Semi-*Pucca* | 71.9 | 92.0 | 74.9 | 28.1 | 8.0 | 25.1 |
| *Kuchcha* | 38.1 | 77.9 | 40.7 | 61.9 | 22.1 | 59.3 |
| *Religion* | | | | | | |
| Christian | 62.9 | 89.3 | 66.8 | 37.1 | 10.7 | 33.2 |
| Hindu | 36.2 | 72.3 | 37.9 | 63.8 | 27.7 | 62.1 |
| Others* | 50.0 | 97.4 | 60.5 | 50.0 | 2.6 | 39.5 |
| **Total** | **3954 (53.1)** | **856 (83.3)** | **4810 (57.1)** | **3487 (46.9)** | **124 (12.7)** | **3611 (42.9)** |

* Others include Muslim, Buddhist, Sikh and others.

Among the States, women from Nagaland had the most information about HIV/AIDS (80.3 per cent) followed by Meghalaya (55.0 per cent) and Assam (37.2 per cent) (Table 2.6). Religion and education might have been responsible for such a differential level of HIV/AIDS information. In spite of geographical isolation, Nagaland Christian women had heard of HIV/AIDS and were better informed as compared to Hindu and Christian Assam women.

**Table 2.6:** Percentage Distribution of Respondents, Heard of HIV/AIDS by State, Age, Education, House Type and Religion

| | *Assasm* | | | *Meghalaya* | | | *Nagaland* | | |
|---|---|---|---|---|---|---|---|---|---|
| | *Heard* | *Not Heard* | *Total* | *Heard* | *Not Heard* | *Total* | *Heard* | *Not Heard* | *Total* |
| *Age* | | | | | | | | | |
| 15-19 | 30.4 | 69.6 | 56 | 35.0 | 65.0 | 60 | 88.9 | 11.1 | 54 |
| 20-29 | 47.1 | 52.9 | 1134 | 61.8 | 38.2 | 1237 | 80.6 | 19.4 | 1103 |
| 30-39 | 32.4 | 67.6 | 1176 | 53.9 | 46.1 | 947 | 82.9 | 17.1 | 1061 |
| 40-44 | 27.8 | 72.2 | 550 | 43.0 | 57.0 | 507 | 73.5 | 26.5 | 536 |
| *Education* | | | | | | | | | |
| Illiterate | 8.3 | 91.7 | 1345 | 27.0 | 73.0 | 855 | 43.3 | 56.7 | 598 |
| 1-5 Class | 34.1 | 65.9 | 419 | 59.0 | 41.0 | 819 | 83.6 | 16.4 | 207 |
| 6-9 Class | 61.1 | 38.9 | 612 | 69.4 | 30.6 | 779 | 88.8 | 11.2 | 780 |
| 10+ Class | 84.4 | 15.6 | 540 | 86.9 | 13.1 | 298 | 92.9 | 7.1 | 1169 |
| *Type of House* | | | | | | | | | |
| *Pucca* | 66.8 | 33.2 | 196 | 87.6 | 12.4 | 442 | 89.0 | 11.0 | 100 |
| Semi-*Pucca* | 61.7 | 38.3 | 532 | 69.1 | 30.9 | 1469 | 88.4 | 11.6 | 1151 |
| *Kuchcha* | 28.6 | 71.4 | 2188 | 13.2 | 86.8 | 834 | 73.5 | 26.5 | 1502 |
| *Religion* | | | | | | | | | |
| Christian | 25.3 | 74.7 | 150 | 54.9 | 45.1 | 2588 | 80.3 | 19.7 | 2731 |
| Hindu | 37.9 | 62.1 | 2729 | 37.8 | 62.2 | 45 | 50.0 | 50.0 | 6 |
| Others* | 37.8 | 62.2 | 37 | 63.6 | 36.4 | 118 | 88.2 | 11.8 | 17 |
| Total | 1085 (37.2) | 1831 (62.8) | 2916 (100) | 1514 (55.0) | 1237 (45.0) | 2751 (100) | 2211 (80.3) | 543 (19.7) | 2754 (100) |

* Others include Muslim, Buddhist, Sikh and others.

The analysis indicates that Hindu rural illiterate women living in Assam could be HIV/AIDS "high risk" category in absence of appropriate information to protect themselves.

HIV/AIDS communication must take this finding into consideration while designing any campaign.

**Sources of HIV/AIDS Information**

The respondents were asked to identify sources of information or persons from whom they had heard about HIV/AIDS. For this purpose multiple information sources were indicated like electronic and print media, health workers, school, friends, family including husband. Table 2.7 shows that both radio and television had provided maximum information to more than 65 per cent women in Assam and 49.4 per cent radio and 25.2 per cent television in Meghalaya. In case of Nagaland, this figure dropped to 38.7 per cent radio and 18.2 per cent television. It seems that electronic media reach decreases as one moves from geographically accessible to inaccessible areas in North-Eastern region. Print media (newspapers and magazines) more or less gave an identical picture in providing information though ability of print media to reach women was much lower than that of electronic media. Slogans/pamphlets and posters seemed quite effective in inaccessible States like Nagaland where 42.3 per cent women came to know about HIV/AIDS through these means. Health-workers including doctors had minor role in providing information about HIV/AIDS. Interpersonal communication among friends and relatives including husband remained single most important source of information about HIV/AIDS in these States. In Nagaland, 92.7 per cent respondents reported having heard of HIV/AIDS through interpersonal communication followed by Meghalaya (76.6 per cent) and Assam (37.8 per cent). In absence of electronic and print media, interpersonal communication seems to be the dominant mode of sharing and exchanging information in a State like Nagaland.

It is suggested that healthcare workers must not be utilized as prime movers and source of information of HIV/AIDS in North-Eastern region. Also State specific communication strategy should be designed to reach to women in their early age.

**Table 2.7:** Percentage Distribution of the Respondents Aware of HIV/AIDS by Sources of Information

| *Source of Information* | *States* | | | | | | | | | *Grand Total* |
|---|---|---|---|---|---|---|---|---|---|---|
| | *Assam* | | | *Meghalaya* | | | *Nagaland* | | | |
| | *Rural* | *Urban* | *Total* | *Rural* | *Urban* | *Total* | *Rural* | *Urban* | *Total* | |
| Radio | 66.8 | 59.0 | 66.1 | 46.2 | 73.7 | 49.4 | 40.7 | 33 | 38.7 | 48.2 |
| TV | 62.3 | 97.0 | 65.5 | 17.8 | 81.7 | 25.5 | 13.1 | 32.4 | 18.7 | 31.1 |
| Newspaper | 32.6 | 58.0 | 34.9 | 17.8 | 49.7 | 21.5 | 21.5 | 26 | 22.7 | 25.1 |
| Magazines | 17.7 | 30.0 | 18.8 | 4.3 | 41.7 | 8.6 | 10.4 | 21.9 | 13.4 | 13.1 |
| Slogan/Pamphlet/Posters | 10.2 | 14.0 | 10.5 | 16.1 | 40.6 | 18.9 | 41.6 | 44.2 | 42.3 | 27.8 |
| Doctors | 2.7 | 0.0 | 2.5 | 1.2 | 10.3 | 2.2 | 8.2 | 11.5 | 9.1 | 5.4 |
| Health-Worker | 2.7 | 1.0 | 2.6 | 2.1 | 1.7 | 2.0 | 7.4 | 10.0 | 8.1 | 4.9 |
| Friends/Relative | 39.3 | 23.0 | 37.8 | 79.4 | 55.4 | 76.6 | 95.6 | 84.3 | 92.7 | 75.2 |
| School Teachers | 1.6 | 1.0 | 1.6 | 1.3 | 0.0 | 1.1 | 4.3 | 5 | 4.5 | 2.8 |
| Community Meeting | 1.2 | 0.0 | 1.1 | 1.3 | 3.4 | 1.6 | 13.7 | 13.1 | 13.6 | 7.0 |
| Husband | 43.7 | 25.0 | 41.9 | 14.2 | 12.6 | 14 | 37.4 | 34.8 | 36.7 | 30.7 |
| **Total** | **985** | **100** | **1085** | **1339** | **175** | **1514** | **1630** | **581** | **2211** | **4810** |

* Percentages do not add up to 100 due to multiple responses.

**Table 2.8:** Percentage Distribution of the Respondents by Mode of Transmission and Age, Education and Religion

| *Mode of Transmission** | *Age (In years)* | | | | *Education* | | | | *Religion* | | | *Grand Total* |
|---|---|---|---|---|---|---|---|---|---|---|---|---|
| | *15-19* | *20-29* | *30-39* | *40-44* | *Illiterate* | *Class 1-5* | *Class 6-9* | *Class 10* | *Christian* | *Hindu* | *Others* | |
| Male having sex with male (Homo-Sexual) | 15.1 | 23.3 | 21.2 | 22.6 | 16 6 | 10.5 | 20.0 | 31.5 | 18.5 | 35.1 | 26.9 | 22.3 |
| Female having sex with male (Hetero-Sexual) | 61.6 | 72.3 | 68.7 | 66.5 | 58.8 | 66.5 | 68.5 | 76.3 | 72.3 | 60.5 | 79.8 | 69.9 |
| Needles/ blades/skin puncture | 39.5 | 37.1 | 37.3 | 34.6 | 19.8 | 18.5 | 34.0 | 53.2 | 35.3 | 42.5 | 33.7 | 36.8 |
| Mother to Child | 23.3 | 29.5 | 27.6 | 26.4 | 16.1 | 10.3 | 24.6 | 43.5 | 26.7 | 33.9 | 25.0 | 28.2 |
| Blood Transfusion | 33.7 | 36.7 | 37.4 | 36.2 | 17.8 | 14.5 | 33.3 | 56.4 | 36.5 | 37.7 | 39.4 | 36.9 |
| Others | 0.0 | 0.7 | 1.2 | 0.7 | 0.2 | 0.4 | 0.9 | 1.2 | 0.8 | 0.9 | 0.0 | 0.9 |
| Do not know | 26.7 | 19.0 | 18.7 | 22.0 | 32.7 | 27.4 | 21.4 | 9.9 | 17.1 | 28.8 | 11.5 | 19.5 |
| **Total** | **86** | **2188** | **1771** | **765** | **602** | **799** | **1608** | **1801** | **3653** | **1053** | **104** | **4810** |

* Percentage does not add up to 100 due to multiple responses.

### Knowledge about Mode of HIV/AIDS Transmission

It seems there is a strong "belief" or "knowledge" among women that HIV/AIDS infection is transmitted through heterosexual sex. Though there are inter-state variations, about 60 per cent across three States believed that HIV/AIDS are transmitted through heterosexual sex (Table 2.8). Table 2.9 shows that 86.9 per cent or six out of seven urban women in Meghalaya believed so. Except in Meghalaya, women in two other States indicated that use of common needle/blade or skin puncture was second most common mode by which HIV/AIDS infection was transmitted. It is difficult to explain why it was low 17.2 per cent in Meghalaya whereas in Assam 42.3 per cent and 47.6 per cent in Nagaland (Table 2.9).

The third important mode of transmission of HIV/AIDS is due to blood transfusion. Belief that the infection is passed from mother to child was significant in the States of Assam and Nagaland (34.0 per cent and 37.2 per cent respectively), but fairly low in Meghalaya (Table 2.9). The analysis shows inter-state differences in the knowledge thereby suggesting State specific communication strategy to control HIV/AIDS spread in the region.

### HIV/AIDS Cure and Prevention

Out of the sample of 8421, only 4810 or 57.1 per cent had heard of HIV/AIDS. The question "Do you think HIV/AIDS is curable disease?" was asked to all those respondents who had indicated that they had heard of HIV/AIDS. According to Table 2.10, only 9.5 per cent believed that HIV/AIDS was curable, highest being in Nagaland (17.0 per cent). Hence, it is suggested that positive communication should be laid emphasis upon and therefore, communication strategies must be targeted on the issue of cure and "fear" should not be created among the women who are aware of non-curability of HIV/AIDS infection. Instead, preventive aspects should be highlighted and adoption of safe sex should be promoted and communicated.

Table 2.11 shows that women were aware of different methods of HIV/AIDS control by varying degrees in three

States. "Safe sex" seemed to be known to 67.4 per cent women as sure means of HIV/AIDS prevention. However, it is doubtful whether respondents really knew the actual method to be adopted for safe sex.

Table 2.11 shows only 32.3 per cent or just above half the respondents indicated use of condom. Significant inter-state and rural-urban variations were observed in the use of condom for safe sex, lowest being in Meghalaya (13.9 per cent). Over 37 per cent women knew that HIV/AIDS infection could be prevented by transfusion of tested blood and use of sterilized needles and syringes. However, only 20 per cent knew that avoiding pregnancy among HIV/AIDS infected persons could prevent HIV/AIDS. More or less same number of women did not know any preventive measures across three States (Table 2.11). Both inter-state and rural-urban differences were observed in which Meghalaya women reported least awareness of various preventive measures against HIV/AIDS except safe sex. It seems communication focus should be targeted towards actual preventative measures especially use of condom for safe sex.

## Misconceptions about Mode of HIV/AIDS Transmission

Almost one-third of respondents had misconceptions as to how HIV/AIDS is transmitted among human beings highest being 49.5 per cent in Nagaland (Table 2.12). Kissing was considered as one of the modes by HIV/AIDS could be transmitted (24.3 per cent) followed by modes like "sharing clothes" (21.5 per cent) and "sharing kitchen utensils" (22.3 per cent) (Table 2.13). In the same order even stepping on urine/stool, (21.2 per cent) and mosquito/flea or bedbug bites (23.1 per cent) believed to infect a person (Table 2.13). It seems all known modes of transmissions related to other diseases were thought to be sources of HIV/AIDS infection though inter-state and rural-urban differences were observed. A surprising finding is that, these misconceptions by and large were higher among urban women than rural women. In order to combat misconceptions, specific communication approach is essential.

The same should be woven into the total family planning and HIV/AIDS communication package as well.

## Need for Region Specific Communication Approach

Inter-state and rural-urban differences were observed about HIV/AIDS awareness, prevention methods, media contribution and related misconceptions about HIV/AIDS among three States. Hence, communication approach must take these findings and findings of similar surveys in other North-Eastern States into consideration while designing any communication strategy. Education seems to be the single most important determinant in creating awareness about HIV/AIDS. Communication about HIV/AIDS messages should aim at reducing the existing knowledge gap and bring about desired behavioural changes among people not considered in "high risk" group with special reference to female population of Scheduled Castes and Scheduled Tribes in North-Eastern region. Two specific communication approaches have been suggested to develop State and community specific communication strategy.

### *Female Focused Communication*

Keeping in view that women by and large in North-Eastern region play prominent role in domestic and community activities, a "female focused" communication will have positive impact in controlling HIV/AIDS in the region. The women should be "educated" to remove the misconception, and to persuade their men folks to adopt methods of safe sex. The "safe sex" concept must be incorporated in the family planning programme and media messages must highlight concept of safe sex.

Since women encounter sexual experiences early in their lives, existing means of communication including educational institutions must form a part of an "advocacy group" to promote safe sex targeted to young and adolescent females. Women should be encouraged to persuade their men folks to

**Table 2.9:** Percentage Distribution of the Respondents by Knowledge of Mode of Transmission and State

| *Mode of Transmission** | *States* | | | | | | | | | *Grand Total* |
|---|---|---|---|---|---|---|---|---|---|---|
| | *Assam* | | | *Meghalaya* | | | *Nagaland* | | | |
| | *Rural* | *Urban* | *Total* | *Rural* | *Urban* | *Total* | *Rural* | *Urban* | *Total* | |
| Male having sex with male (Homosexual) | 34.8 | 44.0 | 35.7 | 9.3 | 58.3 | 14.9 | 18.7 | 26.7 | 20.8 | 22.3 |
| Female having sex with male (Heterosexual) | 58.8 | 73.0 | 60.1 | 78.5 | 86.9 | 79.5 | 70.9 | 60.1 | 68.1 | 69.9 |
| Needles/blades/skin puncture | 41.1 | 54.0 | 42.3 | 15.7 | 28.6 | 17.2 | 46.9 | 49.6 | 47.6 | 36.8 |
| Mother to Child | 33.8 | 36.0 | 34.0 | 8.1 | 32.6 | 10.9 | 35.1 | 43.2 | 37.2 | 28.2 |
| Blood Transfusion | 36.3 | 47.0 | 37.3 | 12.7 | 50.3 | 17.0 | 47.7 | 57.1 | 50.2 | 36.9 |
| Others | 0.8 | 2.0 | 0.9 | 0.4 | 0.6 | 0.5 | 0.8 | 1.9 | 1.1 | 0.9 |
| Do not know | 30.9 | 9.0 | 28.8 | 18.8 | 6.9 | 17.4 | 19.6 | 7.2 | 16.3 | 19.5 |
| **Total** | **985** | **100** | **1085** | **1339** | **175** | **1514** | **1630** | **581** | **2211** | **4810** |

* Percentage does not add up to 100 due to multiple responses.

**Table 2.10:** Percentage Distribution of Respondents Knowing about Curability of HIV/AIDS by Residential Location and State

| | *States* | | | | | | | | | *Grand Total* |
|---|---|---|---|---|---|---|---|---|---|---|
| | *Assam* | | | *Meghalaya* | | | *Nagaland* | | | |
| | *Rural* | *Urban* | *Total* | *Rural* | *Urban* | *Total* | *Rural* | *Urban* | *Total* | |
| Curable | 5.2 | 18.0 | 6.4 | 0.6 | 2.9 | 0.9 | 15.2 | 22.0 | 17.0 | 9.5 |
| Not Curable | 79.4 | 61.0 | 75.9 | 79.1 | 90.8 | 80.4 | 69.7 | 63.0 | 68.0 | 73.7 |
| Do not know | 17.4 | 21.0 | 17.7 | 20.3 | 6.3 | 18.7 | 15.1 | 15.0 | 15.1 | 16.8 |
| **Total** | **985** | **100** | **1085** | **1339** | **175** | **1514** | **1630** | **581** | **2211** | **4810** |

**Table 2.11:** Percentage Distribution of the Respondents Aware of Preventive Measure Against HIV/AIDS by Residential Location and State

| *Preventive Measure** | *States* | | | | | | | | | *Grand Total* |
|---|---|---|---|---|---|---|---|---|---|---|
| | *Assam* | | | *Meghalaya* | | | *Nagaland* | | | |
| | *Rural* | *Urban* | *Total* | *Rural* | *Urban* | *Total* | *Rural* | *Urban* | *Total* | |
| Use of condom in each intercourse | 45.9 | 57.0 | 46.9 | 10.2 | 42.3 | 13.9 | 31.8 | 54.9 | 37.9 | 32.3 |
| Safe Sex | 59.1 | 74.0 | 60.5 | 67.3 | 67.4 | 67.3 | 69.3 | 75.7 | 71.0 | 67.4 |
| Check blood prior to transfusion | 39.7 | 41.0 | 39.8 | 11.4 | 48.6 | 15.7 | 49.9 | 57.1 | 51.8 | 37.7 |
| Sterilize needles and syringes for injection | 39.1 | 41.0 | 39.3 | 15.7 | 38.9 | 18.4 | 51.8 | 57.3 | 53.2 | 39.1 |
| Avoid pregnancy when having AIDS | 26.1 | 22.0 | 25.7 | 6.7 | 20.0 | 8.3 | 26.5 | 24.6 | 26.0 | 20.4 |
| Others | 0.5 | 0.0 | 0.5 | 0.7 | 0.6 | 0.7 | 1.2 | 0.0 | 0.9 | 0.7 |
| Do not know | 33.0 | 13.0 | 31.2 | 25.9 | 6.3 | 23.6 | 24.9 | 10.0 | 21.0 | 24.1 |
| **Total** | **985** | **100** | **1085** | **1339** | **175** | **1514** | **1630** | **581** | **2211** | **4810** |

* Percentage does not add up to 100 due to multiple responses.

**Table 2.12:** Percentage Distribution of the Respondents having Misconceptions about Mode of Transmission of HIV/AIDS by Residential Location and State

| *Misconception* | *States* | | | | | | | | | *Grand Total* |
|---|---|---|---|---|---|---|---|---|---|---|
| | *Assam* | | | *Meghalaya* | | | *Nagaland* | | | |
| | *Rural* | *Urban* | *Total* | *Rural* | *Urban* | *Total* | *Rural* | *Urban* | *Total* | |
| Having Misconception | 24.0 | 34.0 | 24.9 | 16.8 | 38.3 | 19.3 | 48.5 | 52.3 | 49.5 | 34.4 |
| No Misconception | 76.0 | 66.0 | 75.1 | 83.2 | 61.7 | 80.7 | 51.5 | 47.7 | 50.5 | 65.5 |
| **Total** | **985** | **100** | **1085** | **1339** | **175** | **1514** | **1630** | **581** | **2211** | **4810** |

**Table 2.13: Percentage Distribution of the Respondents having Misconceptions about Mode of Transmission of HIV/AIDS by Residential Location and State**

| *Types of Misconception** | *States* | | | | | | | | | *Grand Total* |
|---|---|---|---|---|---|---|---|---|---|---|
| | *Assam* | | | *Meghalaya* | | | *Nagaland* | | | |
| | *Rural* | *Urban* | *Total* | *Rural* | *Urban* | *Total* | *Rural* | *Urban* | *Total* | |
| Shaking Hands | 1.9 | 5.0 | 2.2 | 5.5 | 14.9 | 6.5 | 22.9 | 23.9 | 23.2 | 13.2 |
| Hugging | 7.7 | 10.0 | 7.9 | 7.3 | 17.7 | 8.5 | 25.5 | 25.6 | 25.5 | 16.2 |
| Kissing | 16.1 | 17.0 | 16.2 | 13.0 | 29.7 | 14.9 | 35.2 | 33.0 | 34.6 | 24.3 |
| Sharing Cloths | 11.9 | 15.0 | 12.2 | 6.9 | 16.6 | 8.1 | 36.4 | 31.7 | 35.2 | 21.5 |
| Sharing Kitchen Utensils | 13.2 | 14.0 | 13.3 | 6.1 | 12.0 | 6.8 | 38.2 | 35.3 | 37.4 | 22.3 |
| Stepping on Urine or Stool | 10.3 | 16.0 | 10.8 | 4.0 | 7.4 | 4.4 | 38.0 | 37.7 | 37.9 | 21.2 |
| Mosquito, Flea or Bedbug bites | 9.5 | 14.0 | 10.0 | 5.3 | 20.6 | 7.1 | 39.0 | 43.7 | 40.6 | 23.1 |
| **Total** | **985** | **100** | **1085** | **1339** | **175** | **1514** | **1630** | **581** | **2211** | **4810** |

* Percentage does not add up to 100 due to multiple responses.

use condom for safe sex and sex denial to men without condom use should be advocated.

### *Emphasis on Interpersonal Communication*

In all the three States interpersonal communication, in which husbands and other relatives seem to provide a great deal of information to women. Due to limited reach of mass media in inaccessible areas, interpersonal communication remains a prime mode of sharing and exchanging views of ideas. Hence, it is suggested that apart from electronic and print media, interpersonal communication and use of posters, hoarding and other existing locally popular means must form an integral part of communication strategy. Efforts should be made to utilize health-workers including doctors in creating awareness of HIV/AIDS who are currently least involved in promoting health care.

## REFERENCES

Anonymous (2000), *Communication Needs Assessment for Developing IEC Strategy for HIV/AIDS Awareness and Control in Gujarat.* Ahmedabad: TALEEM Research Foundation (*Unpublished Draft Report*).

Anonymous (a) (2000), *Rapid Household Survey RCH Project Phase I (1998) Assam.* Ahmedabad: TALEEM Research Foundation.

Anonymous (b) (2000), *Rapid Household Survey RCH Project Phase I (1998) Meghalaya.* Ahmedabad: TALEEM Research Foundation.

Anonymous (c) (2000), *Rapid Household Survey RCH Project Phase I (1998) Nagaland.* Ahmedabad: TALEEM Research Foundation.

# 3

# Health Communication Needs in Madhya Pradesh

*Arbind Sinha*

## Introduction

The Government of India has focused on improving and expanding rural health infrastructure under National Rural Health Mission in order to provide quality healthcare service to rural population[1].

A major factor for many of the health centres in the rural and tribal areas not functioning well is due to a disproportionate emphasis on the establishment of curative centres (dispensaries, hospitals, institutions for specialist treatment) in the urban areas of the country, while a vast majority of those seeking medical relief live in rural areas. However, financial and technical support from the World Bank helped some of the States implement Health Systems Development project to strengthen its rural health system. Yet, despite best efforts and considerable investments, the benefits of the improved and expanded health systems did not penetrate to the weaker sections of society as expected, due to the lack of awareness about health services among the target population. It is in such a situation that the role of Information, Education and Communication (IEC) becomes unquestionable.

IEC has remained an integral part of National Health and Family Welfare Programmes in India since the very beginning. India recognized its importance and evolved a strategy to organize need-based IEC for various National and State health programmes. Understanding health communication needs of the people is a first step to evolving appropriate IEC, and Madhya Pradesh was one of the States use IEC to take healthcare to rural areas.

**Madhya Pradesh and IEC**

The State of Madhya Pradesh (MP) provided primary and secondary level health care services in rural areas through its network of 8741 sub-centres, 1193 PHCs, 229 Community Health Centres and 36 district hospitals (Annual Report on the Public Health and Family Welfare 2000-01). With initiative from the Ministry of Health and Family Welfare, Government of India (New Delhi), a State Health IEC Bureau was established in Madhya Pradesh in the year 1995 to strengthen public health and family welfare related IEC activities and to give these activities a professional orientation.

The present paper discusses Health Communication Needs of the people of Madhya Pradesh and functioning of IEC in the State. It is based on:

- Study of communication needs of the people in Madhya Pradesh,
- Study of knowledge and skill for IEC functions among the human power involved in IEC efforts,
- Examination of access, acceptability, effectiveness, and relevance of media used in IEC,
- Assessment of the training needs of IEC functionaries and other service providers at different levels and its prospects, and
- Recommendation to meet the IEC need of different players.

**Methodology**

The study was initiated after detailed discussions with all the officials concerned with the IEC and Madhya Pradesh Basic Health Services Project at the State Headquarters. It covered six identified districts—Badwani, Mandla, Nimach, Sheopur, Sidhi, and Tikamgarh, representing six geo-cultural regions of

Madhya Pradesh in order to obtain comprehensive data on the functioning of IEC at the district and sub-district level. A large-scale survey in 24 villages in six districts was carried out for understanding of the communication needs at the grassroots level. In each village a Group Discussion (GD) was organised with the villagers.

With the help of multi-stage sampling—two PHC zones in each district were selected.

At the third level, one village having sub-centre (sub-centre village) and another relatively remote village without any sub-centre were selected from each of the selected PHC zone (Table 3.1). From each of these villages, a sample of 40 was covered. Approximately 25 women and 15 men randomly from poorer strata of the society (villagers' perception) were taken from each village. Two villages from original sample were changed due to unavoidable circumstances. The fieldwork was conducted during the period May 20-July 5, 2001.

**Table 3.1:** List of Regions, Districts and Villages covered under Study

| *Sl. No.* | *Geo-Cultural Regions* | *Districts in the Region (selected district highlighted)* | *Study Villages* |
|---|---|---|---|
| 1. | Baghelkhand | Rewa, Satna, Shahdol, **Sidhi**, Umaria | 1. Barambawa 2. Baniatola 3. Veldah 4. Karanpur |
| 2. | Bundelkhand | Chattarpur, Damoli, Datia, Panna, Sagar, **Tikamgarh** | 1. Ahar 2. Lalwadi Khas 3. Degora 4. Kharoi |
| 3. | Chambal | Bhind, Guna, Gwalior, Morena, **Sheopur**, Shivpuri | 1. Khakhir Kher 2. Baad 3. Ajapura 4. Mau |
| 4. | Mahakaushal | Balaghat, Betul, Chhindwara, Dindori, Harda, Hoshangabad, Jabalpur, Katni, **Mandla**, Narsimhapur, Seoni | 1. Alipur 2. Dhatura 3. Singodha 4. Deohar |
| 5. | Malwa | Bhopal, Dewas, Dhar, Indore, Jhabua, Mandsaur, **Nimach**, Raisen, Rajgarh, Ratlam, Sehore, Shahjapur, Ujjain, Vidhisha | 1. Hatunia 2. Hadi Pipalia 3. Dehpur 4. Garwala |
| 6. | Nimar | **Badwani**, Khandwa, Khargone | 1. Babdad 2. Hindli 3. Ausada 4. Megha |

**Data from Service Providers**: Communication needs of the service providers were ascertained by interviewing the entire rank and file of personnel involved in IEC operation in the State—management personnel, executives and field organizers in the State Health Department who were directly or indirectly associated with operation of IEC in the State, officials of Strategic Planning Unit, MPBHSP-Phase III, DSU-Bhopal and State IEC Bureau.

The study team had open group discussions and individual consultations with IEC officials and their counter parts from all the 45 districts. District Training Centres of Madhya Pradesh who participated in three regional workshops at Indore, Jabalpur and Gwalior. Detailed discussions with them gave the study team a perspective of the structure and the functioning of the IEC, and the communication needs of the service providers.

Thus, the three methods-detailed discussion with the IEC functionaries, Group Discussion (GD) with the villagers in selected 24 villages, and survey among the selected respondents in the villages gave a deeper understanding of the health communication needs of the State. The study[2] took care of the 'felt needs' as well as 'observed needs'.

## Background Characteristics of the Respondents

### *Age-Sex Distribution*

A total of 969 respondents were interviewed. The proportion of illiterate female is considerably higher; 65 per cent as compared to 35 per cent of the male counterpart. Analysis of data indicates in Table 3.2 that the respondents are evenly distributed across all age groups. One-fourth of the males and females are from the age segment of 25 years or below, while, 27 per cent of the males and 19 per cent of the female respondents belong to the 41 years and above age group. Rest of them (54 per cent males and 44 per cent females) are more or less equitably distributed between the ages 26-40 years.

### *Education and Occupation*

Overall, 65 per cent of the respondents are illiterate. As expected, the proportion of illiterate female is considerably higher (79 per cent) compared to the male (40 per cent). Among the literates, 47 per cent of males and 18 per cent of females have education upto 10th standard. A relatively higher proportion of male (16 per cent) have received education beyond 10th standard as compared to the female (3 per cent). The highest proportion of illiterate respondents hail from Badwani district (86 per cent) and the lowest from Tikamgarh district (51 per cent) with 19 per cent literacy level of 11th standard and above.

### *Occupation*

The data on main occupation (Table 3.1) indicates that overall 49 per cent of the respondents depend on agriculture while 39 per cent of them are unskilled labourers. It merits mention that three-fourth of the women are working. Of them, 36 per cent working women are unskilled workers and another 32 per cent are agricultural labourers. Sidhi district shows higher proportion of agricultural labour (57 per cent) as against the lowest of 25.7 per cent from Badwani district. Service as a main occupation was reported in 6 per cent of the households. However, in Tikamgarh district, service as a main occupation was reported in 14 per cent of the households.

### *Annual Household Income*

Though it is difficult to estimate the income, nearly half (49 per cent) of the households had annual income upto Rs.12,000, while one-fourth of the households had income between Rs.12,001-24,000. On an average, the annual household income is nearly Rs.22,000. The data indicate that average annual household income is highest in Sheopur district where the annual income is around Rs.36,000 and the lowest in Badwani district with Rs.14,000. The average family size, i.e. the total number of males and females in a household is around seven, with nearly equal ratio of males and females.

## MP Villages and the Health Communication Needs

The survey data were suitably supplemented by qualitative data collected from the group discussion and health functionaries, which are presented here under different sub-heads.

**Table 3.2:** Socio-Cultural Background of the Respondents

| *Respondents Background* | *Man-dla* | *Sidhi* | *Tikam-garh* | *Sheo-pur* | *Bad-wani* | *Nim-ach* | *Male* | *Fe-male* | *Total* |
|---|---|---|---|---|---|---|---|---|---|
| **Sex** | | | | | | | | | |
| Male | 36.4 | 33.5 | 38.1 | 30.8 | 36.5 | 36.9 | 100.0 | 0.0 | 35.4 |
| Female | 63.6 | 66.5 | 61.9 | 69.2 | 63.5 | 63.1 | 0.0 | 100.0 | 64.6 |
| **Age** | | | | | | | | | |
| Upto 25 | 25.5 | 22.8 | 21.9 | 26.4 | 24.0 | 34.4 | 24.5 | 26.5 | 25.8 |
| 26-30 | 22.4 | 24.1 | 23.8 | 20.1 | 17.4 | 18.8 | 18.4 | 22.5 | 21.1 |
| 31-35 | 17.0 | 20.9 | 18.1 | 17.0 | 18.0 | 13.8 | 15.5 | 18.5 | 17.4 |
| 36-40 | 11.5 | 13.9 | 13.8 | 13.2 | 19.2 | 10.6 | 14.9 | 13.1 | 13.7 |
| 41 + | 23.6 | 18.3 | 22.4 | 23.3 | 21.4 | 22.4 | 26.7 | 19.4 | 22.0 |
| **Annual Income** | | | | | | | | | |
| Not Mention | 1.2 | 3.2 | 3.1 | 0.6 | 4.8 | 1.3 | 0.9 | 3.2 | 2.4 |
| Upto 12000 | 67.3 | 61.4 | 33.8 | 24.5 | 54.5 | 57.5 | 49.6 | 50.2 | 49.9 |
| 12001-24000 | 16.4 | 15.2 | 28.1 | 35.2 | 28.7 | 25.6 | 22.7 | 26.0 | 24.9 |
| 24001-36000 | 7.3 | 7.0 | 13.1 | 17.0 | 8.4 | 6.3 | 10.5 | 9.4 | 9.8 |
| 36001 + | 7.8 | 13.3 | 22.0 | 22.7 | 3.6 | 9.4 | 16.3 | 11.2 | 13.0 |
| **Education** | | | | | | | | | |
| Illiterate | 56.4 | 66.5 | 51.3 | 71.7 | 85.6 | 58.1 | 39.7 | 78.9 | 65.0 |
| Upto 5 class | 26.1 | 17.1 | 13.1 | 10.1 | 3.6 | 22.5 | 21.3 | 12.1 | 15.4 |
| 6-10 class | 12.1 | 10.8 | 16.3 | 11.3 | 7.8 | 14.4 | 23.0 | 6.1 | 12.1 |
| 11 class + | 5.4 | 5.7 | 19.4 | 6.9 | 3.0 | 5.0 | 16.0 | 2.9 | 7.5 |
| **Main Occupation** | | | | | | | | | |
| Labour | 56.4 | 57.0 | 26.3 | 42.1 | 25.7 | 28.1 | 35.6 | 41.2 | 39.2 |
| Agriculture | 37.6 | 29.7 | 52.5 | 47.2 | 67.1 | 59.4 | 51.3 | 47.8 | 49.0 |
| Service | 2.4 | 6.3 | 13.8 | 5.0 | 4.8 | 3.8 | 6.4 | 5.8 | 6.0 |
| Business | 1.8 | 5.7 | 5.6 | 3.1 | 2.4 | 8.8 | 6.1 | 3.7 | 4.6 |
| Others* | 1.8 | 1.3 | 1.9 | 2.5 | 0.0 | 0.0 | 0.6 | 1.6 | 1.2 |
| **Total Respondent** | **165** | **158** | **160** | **159** | **167** | **160** | **343** | **626** | **969** |

* Others include Petty business, Business, Professional, Student and Unemployed etc.

## Information Needs on Different Health Issues

The most sought after information was in about Malaria, which nearly half of them asked for. It was followed by Immunization (one-third), and HIV/AIDS, Tuberculosis, Diarrhoea and Family Planning (12 to 15 per cent).

Information needs were high in all major health areas in Badwani district; whereas in Mandla the needs were high for Malaria, Immunization, and Family Planning. Sheopur wanted information on Malaria and Immunization but Nimach needed information on Diarrhoea and Family Planning (Tables 3.3 and 3.4).

**Table 3.3:** Information Needs in Health Areas by District

*(Percentage)*

| *Perception and Opinion* | *Mandla* | *Sidhi* | *Tikam-garh* | *Sheo-pur* | *Bad-wani* | *Nimach* | *Total* |
|---|---|---|---|---|---|---|---|
| **Major Information Needs** | | | | | | | |
| Malaria | 33.3 | 36.7 | 41.9 | 55.4 | 62.3 | 47.5 | 46.2 |
| Immunization | 38.8 | 34.2 | 30.6 | 24.0 | 37.8 | 30.0 | 32.7 |
| HIV/AIDS | 14.5 | 13.3 | 17.5 | 15.7 | 3.0 | 29.4 | 15.5 |
| TB | 16.4 | 12.7 | 16.3 | 19.5 | 7.2 | 15.0 | 14.4 |
| Diarrhoea | 7.9 | 8.9 | 7.5 | 3.1 | 32.3 | 24.4 | 14.1 |
| Family Planning | 15.2 | 8.9 | 5.6 | 5.7 | 7.8 | 25.0 | 11.4 |
| **Total** | **165** | **158** | **160** | **159** | **167** | **160** | **969** |

## Awareness and Utilization of Government Health Facilities

Creation of healthcare facilities does not necessarily guarantee better health for the people. There is close correlation between the awareness of health services among people and the provision of quality services. These would determine the final utilization of services by the target group.

The State of Madhya Pradesh merits compliments for the level of awareness it has created about the availability of healthcare facilities in rural areas. Majority of the respondents (86.6 per cent) were aware of the availability of the Government health facilities in nearby surroundings, within ten kilometres of their villages. The analysis presented in Table 3.5 indicates that more males than females were aware of the availability of government health centres, which provides a range of primary healthcare services—Immunization, Malaria detection and treatment, ANC/PNC, Diarrhoea, and Family Planning. The awareness about other National programmes such as Leprosy, Blindness and HIV/AIDS were very low. It requires an aggressive campaign.

**Table 3.4:** Major Information Needs in Health Areas

*(Percentage)*

| *Perception and Opinion* | *Male* | *Female* | *Total* |
|---|---|---|---|
| **Information Needs** | | | |
| Malaria | 45.2 | 46.8 | 46.2 |
| Immunization | 32.4 | 32.8 | 32.7 |
| HIV/AIDS | 25.4 | 10.1 | 15.5 |
| TB | 19.0 | 12.0 | 14.4 |
| Diarrhoea | 15.7 | 13.3 | 14.1 |
| Family Planning | 13.4 | 10.2 | 11.4 |
| ANC/PNC | 0.9 | 14.5 | 9.7 |
| Cancer | 13.4 | 6.5 | 9.0 |
| Leprosy | 11.1 | 6.7 | 8.3 |
| Nausea | 9.3 | 7.5 | 8.2 |
| Blindness | 5.8 | 6.1 | 6.1 |
| Stomach Problems | 8.1 | 5.5 | 6.1 |
| Cough (Throat Problems) | 5.2 | 5.1 | 5.2 |
| Jaundice | 3.8 | 3.8 | 3.8 |
| Cold | 2.0 | 4.3 | 3.5 |
| Breathing Problems | 2.9 | 2.9 | 2.9 |
| Skin Diseases | 3.5 | 2.4 | 2.8 |
| Body Ache | 4.1 | 1.6 | 2.5 |
| Others* | 8.1 | 5.5 | 6.1 |
| **Total No. of Respondents** | **343** | **626** | **969** |

* Others = Ulcer, BP, Lever Problem, Kidney Paralysis, Diabetes, Brain Tumour, Bones etc.

More people got the information when through personal visits. Contribution of the health workers' visits to their doorstep was as low as 19.2 per cent. Relatives and friends were also the sources of information for 16.9 per cent of the respondents. Group Discussion revealed that Aanganwadi workers and Mahila Swasthya Sevika and the Sarpanch were also sources of information. Though majority of the respondents were aware of the availability of Government health centres, more than one-third still preferred private doctors for any kind of sickness.

The tendency of going to the sub-centre oneself and seeking information is more among the villagers of remote villages than the sub-centre villages where they are provide information by the health-workers and health guide—proximity effect.

**Table 3.5:** Awareness about the Availability of Government Health Facilities and Sources of Information

*(Percentage)*

| *Health Facilities* | *Male* | *Female* | *Total* |
|---|---|---|---|
| **Aware of Govt. Health Facilities within 10 km.** | 91.5 | 83.9 | 86.6 |
| **Total No. of Respondents** | **343** | **626** | **969** |
| **Awareness of Health Services*** | | | |
| ANC/PNC | 42.0 | 46.9 | 45.1 |
| Immunization | 80.9 | 77.7 | 78.9 |
| Diarrhoea | 36.9 | 41.7 | 39.9 |
| Pneumonia | 19.1 | 20.0 | 19.7 |
| Malaria | 71.3 | 65.9 | 67.9 |
| TB | 3.2 | 2.1 | 2.5 |
| Leprosy | 2.9 | 1.9 | 2.3 |
| Blindness | 3.5 | 1.1 | 2.0 |
| HIV/AIDS | 6.4 | 2.5 | 3.9 |
| Family Planning | 30.9 | 25.7 | 27.7 |
| Others | 25.8 | 28.4 | 27.4 |
| **Source of Information*** | | | |
| Self | 75.2 | 61.3 | 66.5 |
| Relative/Friends | 13.4 | 19.0 | 16.9 |
| Health-Worker/ANM | 17.8 | 20.0 | 19.2 |
| Member of Panchayat/Health Guide | 4.8 | 3.0 | 3.7 |
| Print Materials | 1.6 | 0.9 | 1.1 |
| Others | 5.4 | 11.2 | 9.1 |
| **No. of Respondents aware of Health Facilities** | **314** | **525** | **839** |

* Percentages based on those who are aware of Health Facilities.

***Most Credible Person for Seeking Health Information:*** The most prominent and credible person through whom health-related information can be imparted is doctor (68.7 per cent), highest in Nimach and lowest in Sheopur (Table 3.6). It was followed by ANM/Health-Worker (29.5 per cent) whom they heavily relied upon. Credibility of ANM/Health-Workers is higher among women than among men. The analysis shows that Mahila Swasthya Sangh, Jan Swasthya Sangh and youth organizations are yet to establish wide networking to reach the rural community as they are mentioned by a very small number of both male and female respondents. The remote villages have relied more on Anganwadi Workers, NGOs, relatives and friends, and MSS than sub-centre villages.

**Table 3.6:** Most Creditable Person for Seeking Health Information by District

*(Percentage)*

| *Preference of Sources* | *Mandla* | *Sidhi* | *Tikam-garh* | *Sheo-pur* | *Bad-wani* | *Nimach* | *Total* |
|---|---|---|---|---|---|---|---|
| Doctor | 71.5 | 63.9 | 56.3 | 60.4 | 72.5 | 87.5 | 68.7 |
| ANM/Health-Worker | 16.4 | 29.1 | 31.3 | 25.8 | 42.5 | 31.9 | 29.5 |
| Anganwadi Worker | 5.5 | 5.1 | 5.6 | 7.5 | 12.0 | 2.5 | 6.4 |
| Panchayat Officer | 13.3 | 17.7 | 18.8 | 18.9 | 1.8 | 10.0 | 13.3 |
| NGOs | 6.7 | 8.9 | 16.3 | 13.2 | 0.0 | 0.0 | 7.4 |
| Relative/Friends | 1.8 | 10.1 | 18.1 | 13.2 | 11.4 | 4.4 | 9.8 |
| MSS | 3.0 | 5.7 | 5.0 | 2.5 | 0.0 | 2.5 | 3.1 |
| JSR | 8.5 | 1.9 | 0.6 | 1.9 | 7.2 | 0.6 | 3.5 |
| Others | 13.3 | 16.5 | 15.7 | 6.9 | 1.2 | 0.6 | 9.0 |
| **Total No. of Respondents** | **165** | **158** | **160** | **159** | **167** | **160** | **969** |

***Best Mode of Health Information Dissemination*:** The respondents considered individual discussion the most effective means of communication through which complete information can be imparted (48 per cent). This was followed by group discussion preferred by 38.8 per cent of respondents. Since literacy rate among women is as low as 21 per cent, 35.7 per cent of them preferred posters and hoardings, which uses pictures to illustrate the message. Although radio and television sets have reached the villages, it can be seen from Table 3.7, that electronic media was given low priority, as they are generally used for entertainment programmes. Group discussion also supported the view that majority relied heavily on human channels of communication.

Production of attractive and durable materials and extensive display and distribution were emphasized during the discussion.

The contribution of printed matter is highest in Nimach and lowest in Mandla whereas interpersonal sources are credited highest in Mandla and lowest in Nimach. The preference for printed medium came more from remote villages than sub-centre villages whereas the sub-centre villages preferred group discussion most.

**Table 3.7:** The Best Mode of Health Information Dissemination

*(Percentage)*

| *Perception and Opinion* | *Male* | *Female* | *Total* |
|---|---|---|---|
| **Sources of Information** | | | |
| Radio | 6.7 | 2.7 | 4.1 |
| Television | 12.0 | 10.9 | 11.2 |
| Poster/Hoardings/Pamphlet/Leaflet | 43.1 | 31.6 | 35.7 |
| Campaign/Mela | 21.6 | 15.8 | 17.9 |
| Folk Drama | 14.0 | 13.3 | 13.5 |
| Group discussion | 42.6 | 36.7 | 38.8 |
| Individual discussion | 43.4 | 50.5 | 48.0 |
| Others | 17.8 | 17.4 | 17.5 |
| **Total No. of Respondents** | **343** | **626** | **969** |

***Visit of Health-Workers*:** Health-worker was the major source of inter-personal communication delivery at village level. 52.7 per cent of the respondents were contacted by the male or female health-workers or Anganwadi Workers. While visiting individual homes, these workers imparted information on various health issues. However, the data from group discussions revealed that ANM visits were irregular, except during the polio drive. Table 3.8 indicates that only in 12.8 per cent of the cases did these workers provide information on health issues. They mainly discussed Immunization, Malaria, Family Planning, ANC/PNC and Diarrhoea.

***Visit to Government Health Centre*:** Communication on various aspects of health is not limited to the visit of Multi-Purpose Health-Workers; the villagers do visit health centres and get information themselves. 36.8 per cent of the respondents visited government health centres and got health related information apart from the treatment/advice sought for. Thus, some communication definitely takes place between health centre and the villagers who visit the health centres.

**Table 3.8:** Visit of Health-Workers in last 3 Months and Use of IEC Material

*(Percentage)*

| *Visit and Use of IEC Material* | *Male* | *Female* | *Total* |
|---|---|---|---|
| **Visited by** | | | |
| ANM/MPW (F) | 37.6 | 37.7 | 37.7 |
| MPW (M) | 24.2 | 25.1 | 24.8 |
| Anganwadi Worker | 23.9 | 22.5 | 23.0 |
| **Visited by any Health-Worker** | **53.6** | **52.2** | **52.7** |
| **Type of Information Given** | | | |
| Not visited by any Health-Worker | 46.4 | 47.8 | 47.3 |
| ANC/PNC | 14.3 | 18.1 | 16.7 |
| Immunization | 43.7 | 42.8 | 43.1 |
| Diarrhoea | 14.6 | 17.1 | 16.2 |
| Pneumonia | 4.7 | 7.8 | 6.7 |
| Malaria | 27.1 | 29.1 | 28.4 |
| TB | 0.9 | 1.9 | 1.5 |
| Leprosy | 3.8 | 1.9 | 2.6 |
| Blindness | 0.9 | 1.3 | 1.1 |
| HIV/AIDS | 3.5 | 2.6 | 2.9 |
| Family Planning | 20.4 | 16.9 | 18.2 |
| Others | 12.2 | 10.9 | 11.4 |
| **Use of IEC Materials by Health-Worker** | **16.0** | **11.0** | **12.8** |
| **Type of IEC Materials Used** | | | |
| Not visited by any Health-Worker | 46.4 | 47.8 | 47.3 |
| Not used IEC Materials | 37.6 | 41.2 | 39.9 |
| Used IEC Materials | 16.0 | 11.0 | 12.8 |
| Pamphlets | 12.0 | 8.5 | 9.7 |
| Poster | 7.9 | 5.3 | 6.2 |
| Flip-chart | 0.3 | 1.3 | 0.9 |
| Others | 0.3 | 0.2 | 0.2 |
| Do not remember | 0.9 | 0.6 | 0.7 |
| **Total No. of Respondents** | **343** | **626** | **969** |

***Access to Health Information through Electronic Media***: Analysis in Table 3.9 shows that only 10.3 per cent of the respondents mentioned that they listen to health related messages on radio (16.6 per cent males and 6.9 per cent females). The content of information was Immunization, Family Planning, HIV/AIDS and Malaria. Only few of them mentioned about Diarrhoea, TB, Leprosy, Cancer, and others. Television had slightly higher contribution (15 per cent)—more males than females. The health related messages that they had received through television were Immunization, Family Planning, Malaria, Leprosy and TB. Of course, a few of them did mention receiving information on Blindness, Cancer, Diarrhoea and ANC/PNC.

**Table 3.9:** Major Health Related Messages through Mass Media

*(Percentage)*

| | *Male* | *Female* | *Total* |
|---|---|---|---|
| **Exposure to Radio** | | | |
| Exposure of health messages on radio (out of total) | 16.6 | 6.9 | 10.3 |
| **Type of Messages on Radio*** | | | |
| Immunization | 40.4 | 48.8 | 44.0 |
| Malaria | 22.9 | 20.9 | 22.0 |
| Leprosy | 15.8 | 4.7 | 11.0 |
| HIV/AIDS | 40.4 | 20.9 | 32.0 |
| Family Planning | 52.6 | 30.2 | 43.0 |
| **Total No. of Respondents listen messages on Radio** | **57** | **43** | **100** |
| **Exposure to TV** | | | |
| Exposure of health messages on TV (out of total) | 17.8 | 13.3 | 14.9 |
| **Type of Messages on TV** | | | |
| Immunization | 52.4 | 65.2 | 60.4 |
| Malaria | 23.0 | 36.1 | 30.6 |
| Leprosy | 21.3 | 13.3 | 16.7 |
| HIV/AIDS | 68.9 | 48.2 | 56.9 |
| Family Planning | 57.3 | 31.3 | 42.4 |
| **Total No. of Respondents have watched messages on TV** | **61** | **83** | **144** |

* Percentages based on those have listen messages on Radio.

## Communication Needs

Every component of the health system—the patients, the general public, the social institutions, the support systems, and the health providers, need information on health. The author tried to outline the communication needs of Madhya Pradesh Public Health and Family Planning system—the communication needs of the people as well as the service providers.

### *Communication Needs of the People*

In spite of the fact that the villagers had fairly good awareness in Malaria and Immunization, ANC/PNC and Diarrhoea, they wanted more information on Immunization and Malaria. Other areas where information was required was in HIV/AIDS and Tuberculosis. The study confirms that once you have information, it generates need for getting more information in those areas. The data also indicate that the need for health information is determined by the seriousness of health issues.

The villagers do not consider normal health problems as requiring special attention. The challenge lies in informing the target population about other diseases such as Jaundice, Blindness, Heart Disease and Cholera. The Department of Health needs to organize aggressive campaigns for this. The IEC functionaries as well as the service providers need to pass on complete information on these issues to make the target population aware about normal health problems.

Badwani and Sheopur districts need special IEC drive on Malaria, while Badwani and Mandla should focus more on Immunization. Nimach and Tikamgarh require more efforts to reach the public with information on HIV/AIDS. Similarly, Mandla, Tikamgarh and Sheopur need relatively more information on Tuberculosis. Badwani and Nimach would require more information on Diarrhoea whereas the information level of Nimach and Mandla is higher in the areas of Family Planning.

The health information seeking behaviour of the beneficiaries have a pattern. They seek health information through following three sources:

### *Information through the Human Channel*

The analysis shows that the health-workers made reasonable contribution towards health awareness in the villages. They are also the second most credible source (persons) with 29.5 per cent acceptability among the respondents. Badwani, Nimach and Tikamgarh rated the credibility of health-workers higher than other districts. This workforce should be further trained and equipped with IEC materials, which they do not use very often (only 12 per cent). The villagers are of the opinion that with the help of IEC materials, the health-workers would be able to educate the villagers more effectively.

The villagers consider person-to-person communication the best way of spreading information.

### *Information through Electronic Media*

Although most of the villages have access to Radio and Television sets, their own or available with a member of the community, the contribution of electronic media has been low (only 4 per cent and 11 per cent respectively) against human channel: Individual discussion and group discussion (48 per cent and 39 per cent). The analysis indicates that not much of resources should be invested in mass media; rather these resources should be diverted to strengthen the human channel of communication: In the present day context, it is constituted by ANMs (38 per cent), male health-workers (25 per cent) and Anganwadi Workers (23 per cent).

### *Communication by Visiting Health Centres*

The villagers themselves are on the look out for health information. They usually find this information when they visit the doctors at health centres, and through other IEC materials displayed there. Thus, the health centres are not only places for providing health, but also for dissemination of health information. The villagers have also shown their interest in the print medium like poster, hoarding, pamphlet and leaflets. This situation necessitates strengthening the IEC functioning from the health centres. Print medium such as posters/hoarding/pamphlets/leaflets have also been indicated as source of health information by a substantial proportion of the respondents (36 per cent).

## Communication Needs of the Service Providers

Communication needs of the IEC officials and other service providers were ascertained by individual consultations as well as group discussions with the entire rank and file of officials involved in IEC operation in State, who were directly or indirectly involved in the IEC operation. The study covered IEC officials from all 45 districts and their counterparts in District Training Centres of Madhya Pradesh who participated in three regional workshops. Another exhaustive exercise was done with the doctors at the PHC, CHC and District Hospitals to get an idea of their communication needs. Discussions were also held with the individual CM&HO in study districts. It provided a perspective of the situation and some idea on the structure and functioning of IEC; and the materials, training, and technology needs for the State in terms of communication. These are presented as under:

### *Communication Needs of the IEC Officials*

The communication needs of the State level IEC officials are mostly training on IEC concepts, its organization, and monitoring whereas the district level officials have their own communication needs of understanding the role of IEC in the rural context. They need orientation and skill upgradation on inter-sectoral and intra-sectoral coordination and event management. The need is more in the area of operationalising the IEC activities in the districts. Both the State and district

IEC officials lack a holistic understanding of IEC. In absence of this understanding, they usually endup functioning like a post box, passing on the IEC material received from the Centre or the State to the block level functionaries.

The Block Extension Educators (BEEs) lack understanding in the basics of communication, most of the functionaries at all levels need conceptual clarity in understanding the different elements of health and rural communication, initiative and creativity in IEC.

### *Communication Needs of the Health-Workers*

The ANMs, male health-workers and the Anganwadi workers do understand the importance of IEC and their reliance on person-to-person communication; but very rarely do they get an organized group discussion. Their understanding was limited to information on disease and its consequences, precautions and treatment. They are in need of training on persuasion and motivation. TBAs do come into contact with people and impart knowledge on safe delivery of child and childcare. They need to be equipped with complete and correct information. All of them, however, require regular updating of their knowledge, both for self-confidence and to carry out their duties.

### *Communication Needs of the Medicos*

The communication needs of the service providers from medical side are at a slight variance. The doctors needed to describe the details of various diseases to the patients and their attendants. Thus, they are required to make use of pictorial booklets (made of durable paper or laminated sheets) on major diseases mentioned earlier. With help of these pictorials they can describe the problems more easily. Most of the doctors agreed that work pressure barely allowed enough time for complete explanations about diseases. All of them wanted such IEC materials made available with them for their use, whenever time permits.

## Training Needs and Prospects

The value of training is indisputable. Training is required by all players of development programmes in order to remain up-to-date and learn newer techniques.

### *Training Facilities*

Training on IEC is included in one form or the other in the training programmes organized in Madhya Pradesh. At the State level, it is organized at State Institute of Health Management and Communication (SIHMC) at Gwalior, the nodal agency in Madhya Pradesh to give direction and to set pace of IEC in the State with special emphasis on communication as a whole. At the regional level, three Regional Health and Family Welfare Training Centres (RHFWTCs) at Indore, Jabalpur and Gwalior do organise trainings for IEC personnel at the district level. This responsibility remains to be handled by the District Training Centres. The State has other training venues such as Madhya Pradesh Voluntary Health Association (MPVHA), Indore, and Mahatma Gandhi Institute of Rural Development, Jabalpur. Often, this type of training is coordinated by persons other than IEC experts, mostly medicos. It would be proper if exclusive training programmes are organized and coordinated by persons from IEC cadre.

Group discussions revealed that in most of these training programmes, elements of IEC were weak. It has been reported that communication topics were covered by non-communication persons during the training, and that it discussed more on the clinical and public health problem rather than problem of awareness, content, credibility, and information network. Proper care was required to see that the elements of development communication, rural communication, and health communication were emphasized. A separate committee should have gone through the training syllabus to see that adequate emphasis is given to IEC, where information dissemination is the key word. If it is discussed without mentioning, the process of information reach to the final user and what circumstances it would thrive in, it will not create much impact on the mind of trainees.

The study team suggested a participatory curriculum development for the Training Programme to increase its acceptability among the participants. It could be done in a joint half day session with the trainers and the trainees followed by discussion on the topics agreed upon. This pedagogy of training does not suggest a well-prepared class note but recommends debate on the issues emerging out of the discussion, bringing together the theoretical perspective and practical problems.

## Recommendations

Commensuration with the decentralization policy of the Government of Madhya Pradesh, the IEC should reaffirm its philosophy on promoting community mobilization and community participation in public health and Family Welfare Programmes. The situation demands energizing the workforce, enhancing the knowledge and sharpening the skill through proper training/orientation of the staff towards the shift in paradigm—from creating awareness to information, education and motivation to meet the needs of the IEC operations in the State. The pyramid of IEC functionaries from the State to the village needs to be established. The following steps are recommended to strengthen IEC programme in Madhya Pradesh in order to achieve the goal of "quality health for all".

## IEC Workshop for Collectors and CM&HOs

- As part of advocacy, meetings should be organized with the policy-makers and top executives—politicians as well as bureaucrats from all development departments/programmes in the State, which in turn would facilitate smooth functioning of the IEC activities in the State. The advocacy should highlight issues of IEC rather than issues of the programme.
- At district level, the Collectors and the Chief Medical and Health Officers should be involved in the process

of IEC. It is suggested to organize a workshop of the Collectors and CM&HOs. An eminent health communication person should be invited to provide a theoretical perspective of IEC. Field data indicated that wherever the Collector took interest in any of the health-care programme, the results were much better.

### IEC Refresher Training for Staff of State Bureau and SIHMC

- The State Bureau staff was experienced and were capable of handing the task assigned to them but they needed theoretical understanding of communication and IEC, especially in the context of rural communication. Vacant posts should be filled and the new incumbent should be given proper training on IEC.
- They need to understand processes and concerns in IEC material development including message designing, testing, modification, and feedback. They could learn to chalk-out the technical inputs required from consultants.
- The importance of inter-sectoral linkages should be emphasised, in order to help with effective execution of IEC programme in the State.
- The State Bureau required computers for data processing, for creating database, computation and for generating IEC materials. Training on computer operation and computer-based message designing should be organized for them.
- M.P. Swasthya Sanchar, the newsletter from State IEC Bureau was a good initiative. This needed a thrust. The concerned officials in the State Bureau should be trained in the basics of editorial policy and layout.
- The faculty of State Institute of Health Management and Communication (SIHMC) who usually organizes trainings on health communication, should be trained themselves in updating their knowledge of health communication in context of rural health.

## IEC Training for DEMOs and Deputy DEMOs

- The DEMOs and Deputy DEMOs should see the scope of IEC beyond using mass media, posters and handbills. They should shift their paradigm from only creating awareness to motivation and case drive by enriching their knowledge in holistic IEC. The DEMOs and Deputy DEMOs could be educated about Communication Needs Assessment and research methods to conduct it.
- Better understanding of social dynamics in communication and the contribution of the religious leaders, public representative and other opinion leaders would help them execute the programme more effectively. They should be oriented in development communication and development support communication, health communication and use of media—electronic media, print media, folk media, official channel and human channel.
- The strategy for formation of taluka and district level IEC committees with different stakeholders for effective implementation of IEC plan could be part of the training. This would help them in planning, organising and conducting the IEC campaign and also in monitoring the developments.
- The training curriculum could include discussion on focusing the IEC towards the service providers; their professional ethics and the social responsibility. The District IEC Unit required training in computer operation and computer-based design. Training is required for the DEMO and other support staff for handling the audio-visual equipments. Simple operating manuals be prepared and given to the district and block officials. They in turn would organize such refresher course(s) at district for BEEs and Health-Workers and others involved in IEC operation at sub-block level.

## IEC Training for BEEs

- If any single factor is to be blamed for 'not so good' result of IEC in Madhya Pradesh, it is the poor performance of the village level health staff—Sector Supervisor and MPWs. Their numbers were few and they were over burdened with various tasks. In this situation the meaningful use of the available staff and bringing socially concerned persons in the village into IEC fold are alternatives. The whole emphasis could be on resource mobilisation and its optimum utilisation. They should learn to identify people's resistance and plan their strategy accordingly.
- Display of IEC materials at the health-centres were a major source of information for the villagers. More people visited the health-centres themselves to get some health-related information. Thus, more prominent display of wall painting, posters and hoardings with more pictorial depiction of doctor centric health information should be placed. For tribal regions, doctor centric IEC materials with powerful visual appeal should be properly displayed at school buildings, Panchayat halls and grocery shops in the villages. Durable material should be used for these IEC posters.
- The felt need of the villagers of Madhya Pradesh had been the human channel in the form of person-to-person communication followed by group discussion and print medium—poster, hoarding, and pamphlets.
- BEEs needed to know how to use IEC for informing, educating and motivating the village volunteers to come forward and help the programme at their level.

## Private Initiative

- The study brought out the idea of private initiative in the organisation of IEC at district level. The response was encouraging, although one cannot gauge the private industry's interest in the welfare sector. The study suggested that on experimental basis the IEC task in one or two districts or part of the district be made open for private initiative by a non-government organization or private institution with established credential. They should be given all the tasks and the fund earmarked for the district.

## NOTES

1. In rural areas health-services are provided through the network of health and family welfare delivery system. An extensive network of community health-centres, primary health-centres and centres has been set up to provide primary health care at the grassroots level. One female and a male multi-purpose worker covering a population of 5,000 in plain areas and 3,000 in hilly, tribal, backward and difficult terrain areas manage each sub-centre.
   Each Primary Health Centre is staffed with medical officer, pharmacist, staff nurse, female multi-purpose worker, health educator, laboratory technician, female health assistant, male health assistant each, besides other four or five Ministerial staff, for covering a population of 30,000 in the plain areas and 20,000 in tribal and difficult terrain areas. Similarly, each Community Health Centre is staffed with medical specialist, surgical specialist, child specialist, and gynaecologist each, besides 25 other para-medical and Ministerial staff. It has 30 indoor beds, well-equipped laboratory and X-ray facility. It covers 80,000 to 1,20,000 rural populations.
2. **Systems Study**—Study of IEC management of MP Health IEC Bureau. It also included functioning of IEC at district, block, and sub-block level. IEC was seen in totality with the healthcare scenario at various levels.
   **IEC Needs**—IEC needs at the State, district, and the villages. At the district and block level, the DEMO or Deputy DEMO or the BEE looking after the IEC activities in the district were approached to identify communication needs, the operational problems, and for suggestions to rectify them. Village level data came from survey conducted in 24 villages of six districts. Thus, the needs expressed by the management, executives, implementers, and target groups themselves completed the line of investigation from the top to bottom.
   **IEC in Public Health and Family Welfare in M.P.**—Detailed discussions with all levels of the officials and functionaries on how to revitalise IEC activities in the State.

## REFERENCES

Anonymous, (1998a), *Report of the "Independent Commission on Health in India"*. New Delhi : Voluntary Health Association of India.

*Annual Report* (Anonymous) (2001), Annual Report of the Department of Public Health and Family Welfare (2000-01). Bhopal: Government of Madhya Pradesh.

*Bureau Document* (Anonymous) (1998), Report on the Working of State IEC Bureau. Bhopal : State Health IEC Bureau.

Goodenough, Ward Hunt, (1963), *Cooperation in Change*, pp. 17-54. New York : Russell Sage Foundation.

Government of India, (New Delhi), *Assistance to the States for Establishing an IEC Bureau (Guidelines)*. New Delhi : Ministry of Health and Family Welfare.

JICA and FPAI, (New Delhi) *Report on the Role of IEC on RCH Behaviour Change (A Case Study)*. Bhopal : Japan International Cooperation Agency and Family Planning Association of India.

Murthy, G.V.S. (1997), Human Resource Development in Community Ophthalmology. *Indian Journal of Community Health*, Vol. 3(2): 43-51.

Quebral, Nora C. (1988), *Development Communication*. Philippines: University of the Philippines.

Sinha, Arbind (1999), *Health Communication in India: The Challenge*. New Delhi: DANIDA.

# 4

# Impact of Social Marketing on Condom Promotion for HIV/AIDS Prevention

*Mitali Chakrabarty* and *Dhanji B. Patel*

## Introduction

The awareness of HIV/AIDS has risen to some extent among people in India since the first reported case in 1986. The question is, to what extent are people aware about the infection? Even today, an HIV/AIDS infected person is stigmatized and discriminated by friends, families, relatives and society in workplace and also in health-care systems. 'HIV-related stigma and discrimination remains an enormous barrier to effectively fighting the HIV and AIDS epidemic' (http://www.avert.org/aidsstigma.htm).

In India, 5.1 million people were HIV/AIDS infected as estimated in 2003 (NACO, 2005, p. 1 and Gujarat State AIDS Control Society, 2005, p. 1). Gujarat has seen an alarming increase in the incidence of HIV/AIDS. HIV/AIDS is spreading to rural areas and to the general population (www.developmentinaction.org/newspages/index/67.php). This being a serious concern, the Government of Gujarat created an autonomous organization, namely Gujarat State AIDS Control Society (GSACS) for controlling HIV/AIDS. GSACS has identified some high-risk HIV/AIDS prevalence areas in Gujarat.

The effectiveness of condom for prevention of HIV/AIDS has been the subject of research for over a decade. Research studies have found that the consistent use of condoms during sexual intercourse results in 80 per cent reduction in HIV incidence (Weller and Davis, 2003). Condom social marketing has raised the condom use in some countries (Spring 1998, Vol. 18, No. 3). DKT, a social marketing organization has implemented condom promotion programme in the high-risk areas of Gujarat for preventing HIV/AIDS.

The present paper aims to assess the impact of social marketing on usage of condom for reducing HIV/AIDS.

## Methodology

The paper is based on a study commissioned by DKT India in 2006 to assess the impact of social marketing on availability, acceptability and accessibility of condom in the selected high-risk areas in Gujarat.

A multi-stage sampling design was followed to achieve the objectives of the study.

## Sampling

The various condom promotion programmes are being conducted in the high risk areas (both rural and highway sites) of 11 districts in Gujarat as identified by GSACS. Out of these high-risk sites, 40 per cent of the rural high-risk sites have been selected in proportion to the number of sites from each district. This way, a total of 62 sites has been selected. Similarly, highway sites have been selected subject to minimum of one site and maximum of three from each district. Thus, a total of 22 highway sites have been selected (Table 4.1).

At the second stage of sampling, 10 males in the sexually active age group of 15-54 years have been randomly selected from each rural site. Similarly, five females including commercial sex workers in the age group 15-49 have been randomly selected from each rural site. Thus, a total sample of 620 male respondents and 310 female respondents from rural sites were covered.

Similarly, from each highway high-risk site, five to 10 male truckers have been selected. In the same vicinity, five females including commercial sex-workers in the age group 15-49 have been selected randomly for interview.

Sampling frame for the interview of condom retailers was prepared for each selected site of rural as well as highway areas, after mapping the condom retail sellers.

**Table 4.1:** Distribution of Sample by Sites and Districts

| *Sl. No.* | *District* | *Rural High Risk Sites* | | | *Highway High-Risk Sites* | | |
|---|---|---|---|---|---|---|---|
| | | *Taluka* | *Rural Sites* | *Sample Sites* | *Taluka* | *Sites* | *Sample Sites* |
| 1. | Jamnagar | 5 | 8 | 3 | 1 | 1 | 1 |
| 2. | Junagadh | 6 | 11 | 4 | 1 | 1 | 1 |
| 3. | Rajkot | 5 | 6 | 2 | 2 | 2 | 2 |
| 4. | Surendra-nagar | 6 | 11 | 4 | 2 | 2 | 2 |
| 5. | Kutch | 8 | 34 | 14 | 2 | 2 | 2 |
| 6. | Sabarkantha | 8 | 12 | 5 | 3 | 3 | 2 |
| 7. | Banaskantha | 9 | 17 | 7 | 1 | 1 | 1 |
| 8. | Ahmedabad | 3 | 10 | 4 | 3 | 7 | 2 |
| 9. | Bharuch | 6 | 11 | 4 | 5 | 13 | 3 |
| 10. | Surat | 14 | 33 | 13 | 9 | 11 | 3 |
| 11. | Vadodara | 2 | 5 | 2 | 8 | 14 | 3 |
| | **Total** | **72** | **158** | **62** | **37** | **57** | **22** |

This way a sample size of 797 male respondents in the age group 15-54 years and 420 female respondents of age group 15-49 years were randomly selected from 62 rural sites and 22 highway sites. The sample population includes truck drivers and sex workers, the most vulnerable and high-risk groups for transmitting HIV/AIDS. Out of 797 male respondents, 177 were truck drivers and 619 were community members. In case of 420 women, 391 were community members and 29 were sex-workers. In addition, 236 retailed condom sellers were interviewed.

The respondents were interviewed in person using three types of structured questionnaires. One type of questionnaire was for interviewing males in the age group 15-54 years, the other for interviewing females in the age group 15-49 years and the third one was for interviewing the condom retail sellers.

## Findings

### *Awareness of Condom*

Overwhelming majority of men (97 per cent) and women (92 per cent) were aware of condom and television was found to be the most popular source of awareness (Table 4.2).

**Table 4.2:** Awareness of Condom

| *Awareness* | *Male* | *Female* |
|---|---|---|
| Per cent aware of condom | 97.2 | 91.9 |
| **Total (N)** | **797** | **420** |
| **Awareness by Source*** | | |
| Radio | 36.1 | 30.1 |
| Television | 89.3 | 71.2 |
| Newspaper/Magazine/Books | 45.3 | 25.9 |
| Slogans/Pamphlets/Posters/Hoarding/ POP materials/Sticker | 32.8 | 24.1 |
| Movies/Theatre | 5.7 | 4.9 |
| Doctor | 14.5 | 13.7 |
| Health Centre | 27.1 | 27.2 |
| Community-worker | 4.3 | 9.6 |
| NGO Worker | 23.2 | 16.1 |
| Anganwadi Worker/ Health-Worker | 18.7 | 45.3 |
| Sex Partner | 11.1 | 30.1 |
| Friends/Relatives | 37.9 | 28.5 |
| Government Programme | 0.5 | 1.3 |
| DKT Programmes | 17.2 | 8.3 |
| **Total (N)** | **775** | **386** |

* Multiple Responses.

## Condom Users

Table 4.3 reveals that the reporting of condom users in the present study was found to be higher among truck drivers (74 per cent) as compared to other men belonging to community members (69 per cent). In case of women, the condom usage among sex-workers has been remarkable as all of them were users and 61 per cent of community members reported to be users of condom (Table 4.3). In the group discussions conducted in most of the sampled sites, the males reported that the acceptance of condom has increased largely in last one year. This has been, perhaps due to the implementation of various condom promotion and HIV/AIDS awareness programmes organised by DKT and Government agencies like GSACS.

**Table 4.3:** Condom Users

| *Condom Users/ Non-users* | *Male* | | | *Female** | | |
|---|---|---|---|---|---|---|
| | *Community Members* | *Truck Drivers* | *Total* | *Community Members* | *Sex-Workers* | *Total* |
| User | 68.7 | 74.0 | 69.8 | 60.5 | 100.0 | 63.4 |
| Non-user | 31.3 | 26.0 | 30.2 | 39.5 | 0.0 | 36.6 |
| **Total (N)** | **619** | **177** | **796** | **354** | **29** | **383** |

* Excluding 37 unmarried women (community members) who never had sexual intercourse.

## Reasons for Condom Usage

Table 4.4 presents a positive indication for the programme implementers as majority of the vulnerable groups such as

**Table 4.4:** Reasons for Condom Usage

| *Reasons** | *Male* | | | *Female** | | |
|---|---|---|---|---|---|---|
| | *Community Members* | *Truck Drivers* | *Total* | *Community Members* | *Sex-Workers* | *Total* |
| Avoid Pregnancy | 84.0 | 75.8 | 81.8 | 91.6 | 72.4 | 89.3 |
| Avoid STD | 40.7 | 59.5 | 45.1 | 38.8 | 79.3 | 43.6 |
| Avoid HIV/AIDS | 81.9 | 94.7 | 84.9 | 61.7 | 89.7 | 65.0 |
| Increases Sexual Pleasure | 8.5 | 12.2 | 9.4 | 0.9 | 13.8 | 2.5 |
| Can Perform Sex for Longer Time | 9.4 | 13.7 | 10.4 | 1.9 | 31.0 | 5.3 |
| Easy to Use | 17.6 | 16.8 | 17.4 | 17.8 | 6.9 | 16.5 |
| It is inexpensive/ low cost | 3.1 | 3.8 | 3.2 | 6.1 | 3.4 | 5.8 |
| It is easily available | 12.5 | 7.6 | 11.3 | 9.3 | 10.3 | 9.5 |
| **Total (N)** | **425** | **131** | **556** | **214** | **29** | **243** |

* Multiple Responses.

truck drivers (95 per cent) and sex-workers (90 per cent) have reported using condom to avoid HIV/AIDS. This has been a positive indication for the programme implementers.

### Preferred Brands of Condom

Table 4.5 shows that Nirodh is the most preferred brand among all the condom users except sex-workers, followed by Zaroor and Kohinoor brand. Sex-workers mostly prefer to use Zaroor followed by Kohinoor.

**Table 4.5:** Preferred Brands of Condom

| *Preferred brands among Condom Users* | *Male* | | | *Female** | | |
|---|---|---|---|---|---|---|
| | *Community Members* | *Truck Drivers* | *Total* | *Community Members* | *Sex-Workers* | *Total* |
| Nirodh | 46.1 | 33.6 | 43.2 | 46.3 | 17.2 | 42.8 |
| Delux | 3.8 | 6.9 | 4.5 | 2.8 | 0.0 | 2.5 |
| Kohinoor | 12.0 | 18.3 | 13.5 | 9.8 | 20.7 | 11.1 |
| Kamasutra | 0.9 | 3.8 | 1.6 | 0.9 | 6.9 | 1.7 |
| Zaroor | 31.5 | 32.1 | 31.7 | 31.8 | 34.5 | 32.1 |
| XXX dotted | 5.2 | 6.9 | 5.6 | 1.9 | 6.9 | 2.5 |
| Others | 3.2 | 3.1 | 3.4 | 2.8 | 0.0 | 2.4 |
| Do not know | 0.0 | 2.3 | 0.9 | 3.7 | 13.8 | 4.9 |
| **Total (N)** | **425** | **131** | **556** | **214** | **29** | **243** |

### Reasons for Preference of Condom Brands

The reasons for using most preferred brands of condom such as Nirodh, Zaroor and Kohinoor have been shown in Table 4.6. Nirodh, which is Government-supplied brand, is mostly preferred for free availability (78 per cent among men and 89 per cent among women) (Table 4.5). Men mainly prefer the DKT product Zaroor for it is always available (55 per cent) and women mostly prefer as it is available at a subsidized rate (58 per cent). Kohinoor, is generally preferred by men due to sexual satisfaction (47 per cent) and attractive packaging (41 per cent). Women also mainly prefer Kohinoor brand for sexual satisfaction (44 per cent).

**Table 4.6:** Reasons for Preference of Condom Brands

| *Reasons for most Preferred Brands** | *Nirodh* | | *Zaroor* | | *Kohinoor* | |
|---|---|---|---|---|---|---|
| | *Male* | *Female* | *Male* | *Female* | *Male* | *Female* |
| Available free | 78.3 | 88.5 | 8.6 | 18.0 | 1.3 | 7.4 |
| Available at low cost | 7.7 | 23.1 | 35.1 | 57.7 | 15.5 | 22.2 |
| Always available | 28.2 | 32.7 | 54.9 | 29.5 | 35.2 | 25.9 |
| More satisfaction | 17.1 | 7.7 | 24.0 | 11.5 | 46.7 | 44.4 |
| Easily available | 32.9 | 38.5 | 39.4 | 39.7 | 15.5 | 33.3 |
| Attractive packaging | 0.8 | 0.0 | 21.4 | 17.9 | 41.3 | 14.8 |
| Partner likes | 12.4 | 13.5 | 8.9 | 19.2 | 18.3 | 29.6 |
| Do not know | 1.7 | 1.0 | 0.6 | 1.3 | 2.8 | 14.8 |
| **Total (N)** | **240** | **104** | **175** | **78** | **75** | **27** |

* Multiple Responses.

## Availability of Condom in Retail Shop

A total of 236 retail shops were located in 84 sites where condoms were being sold, out of which, 166 were in rural sites and 70 in highway sites (Table 4.7). Thus, on an average there were three condom retail shops each in rural and highway sites.

**Table 4.7:** Availability of Condom in Retail Shop

| *Number of Retail Shops* | *Rural Site* | *Highway Site* | *Total* |
|---|---|---|---|
| 1-3 | 46.4 | 28.6 | 41.1 |
| 4-6 | 37.9 | 27.2 | 34.7 |
| 7-9 | 9.0 | 27.1 | 14.4 |
| 10+ | 9.0 | 21.5 | 12.5 |
| **Total** | **166** | **70** | **236** |

## Availability of Various Brands

The availability of various brands of condoms at the retail shops has been shown in Table 4.8. Overwhelming majority of the condom retail sellers (98 per cent) reported the availability of condom all the time in their shops, irrespective of rural and highway sites. Zaroor brand of condom has been very popular as more than 80 per cent of the condom retail sellers both in rural as well as in highway sites reported having the brand in stock. The condom retail sellers remarked that brands like XXX dotted (35 per cent) and Kohinoor (32 per cent) are also mostly available as per demand of customers.

**Table 4.8:** Availability of Various Brands in Retail Shops

| | *Rural Site* | *Highway Site* | *Total* |
|---|---|---|---|
| Availability of condoms at the shops all the time | 97.0 | 98.6 | 97.5 |
| **Availability of Brands** | | | |
| Nirodh | 10.8 | 14.3 | 11.9 |
| Delux | 11.4 | 8.6 | 10.6 |
| Kohinoor | 34.3 | 25.7 | 31.8 |
| Kamasutra | 7.2 | 7.1 | 7.2 |
| Masti | 3.0 | 0.0 | 2.1 |
| Ustad | 3.6 | 1.4 | 3.0 |
| Zaroor | 83.7 | 81.4 | 83.1 |
| XXX dotted | 30.7 | 44.3 | 34.7 |
| Moods | 0.6 | 4.3 | 1.7 |
| Durex | 1.2 | 2.9 | 1.7 |
| Wildkats | 0.6 | 2.9 | 1.3 |
| Others* | 16.3 | 25.7 | 19.1 |
| **Total (N)** | **166** | **70** | **236** |

* Others include Rangeela, Luxary, Kobra, Lovely, Josh, Rangeen, Fantastics, Love time, Imports.

## Sale of Various Brands

The sale of various brands as reported by the retailers has been shown in Table 4.9. Zaroor, DKT brand (70 per cent) is the widely sold brand of condom followed by Kohinoor (21 per cent) and XXX dotted (18 per cent).

The men and women during group discussions reported that the availability and accessibility of condoms enhanced greatly in past one year. In almost all the sites irrespective of rural and highway, the people responded that they obtain condom easily from the retail shops, within the range of 0-2 kms.

**Table 4.9:** Sale of Various Brands

| *Sale of Brands* | *Rural Site* | *Highway Site* | *Total* |
|---|---|---|---|
| Nirodh | 6.6 | 8.6 | 7.2 |
| Delux | 6.0 | 4.3 | 5.5 |
| Kohinoor | 20.5 | 21.4 | 20.8 |
| Kamasutra | 3.0 | 2.9 | 3.0 |
| Masti | 0.6 | 0.0 | 0.4 |
| Ustad | 1.2 | 0.0 | 0.8 |
| Zaroor | 72.9 | 64.3 | 70.3 |
| XXX dotted | 16.3 | 22.9 | 18.2 |
| Durex | 0.6 | 0.0 | 0.4 |
| Wildkats | 0.0 | 2.9 | 0.8 |
| Others* | 12.0 | 21.4 | 14.8 |
| **Total (N)** | **166** | **70** | **236** |

* Others include Rangeela, Luxary, Kobra, Lovely, Josh, Rangeen, Fantastics, Love time, Imports.

The Social Marketing Organisation, and AIDS Control Societies have a positive role in raising awareness of people about the utility and availability of condom and awareness about HIV/AIDS. However, the question is how consistently and correctly, condoms are used for performing safe sex?

## Knowledge about Correct Usage of Condom

The various steps in the correct usage of condoms have been categorised into three such as, (i) **handling of condom** (checking expiry date and to open the packet with care so that condom does not tear), (ii) **usage of condom** (enrolling condom on erect male organ before intercourse, condom needs to be withdrawn immediately after ejaculation to avoid spill over of semen in vagina and tip of the condom should be kept between two fingers while unrolling), and (iii) **disposal of condom** (should be knotted before disposal and wrapped in paper for disposal in dustbin).

Among those who were aware of condoms, only 10 per cent of men and 12 per cent of women had correct knowledge of all steps in using condoms (Table 4.10). Both men and women had very poor knowledge of correct disposal of condoms. It is a concern for the programme implementers and for which proper planning is required to expand the awareness about correct usage of condoms.

**Table 4.10:** Knowledge about Correct Usage of Condom

| *Knowledge* | *Men* | | | *Women* | | |
|---|---|---|---|---|---|---|
| | *Community Members* | *Truck Drivers* | *Total* | *Community Members* | *Sex-Workers* | *Total* |
| **Knowledge about Correct Steps in Using Condom** | | | | | | |
| Only about handling condom | 22.3 | 16.1 | 20.9 | 10.4 | 13.8 | 10.6 |
| Only about usage of condom | 7.3 | 15.5 | 9.2 | 10.1 | 13.8 | 10.4 |
| Only about disposal of condom | 0.0 | 0.0 | 0.0 | 2.8 | 0.0 | 2.6 |
| Both handling and usage | 25.0 | 29.3 | 25.9 | 14.6 | 37.9 | 16.3 |
| Both handling and disposal | 1.8 | 2.3 | 1.9 | 6.2 | 10.3 | 6.5 |
| Both usage and disposal | 1.0 | 1.7 | 1.2 | 1.4 | 6.9 | 1.8 |
| Knowledge about all correct steps | 10.6 | 9.7 | 10.4 | 11.5 | 13.8 | 11.7 |
| No knowledge about any correct step | 32.0 | 25.2 | 30.5 | 43.0 | 3.4 | 40.1 |
| **Total (N)** | **601** | **174** | **775** | **357** | **29** | **386** |

## Regular Usage of Condoms

Though 70 per cent of men and 63 per cent of women reported using condoms (Table 4.3) however, condom usage during each sexual intercourse is not so encouraging, particularly in case of men (31 per cent) (Table 4.11). Reporting of condom users during each intercourse was higher among vulnerable groups such as truckers (48 per cent) and sex-workers (79 per cent) as compared to community members (Table 4.11).

**Table 4.11:** Regular Usage of Condoms

| | *Men* | | | *Women* | | |
|---|---|---|---|---|---|---|
| | *Community Members* | *Truck Drivers* | *Total* | *Community Members* | *Sex-Workers* | *Total* |
| Condom users during each intercourse | 26.1 | 48.1 | 31.3 | 48.1 | 79.3 | 51.9 |
| **Total (N)** | **425** | **131** | **556** | **214** | **29** | **243** |

The most common reasons mentioned for irregular condom usage by men were that, 'they do not require using condoms while having sex with their wives' and 'wives do not like to have sex using condom'. The study reveals that the truck drivers and sex-workers tend to use condoms while having sex with paid partners or clients. However, they had been reluctant to use condom with their spouse. Thus, there has been a need to stress continued effort in regular use of condom to prevent the spread of HIV/AIDS.

During the fieldwork, some people (both men and female) reported that they hesitated to buy condoms due to fear of negative attitude of people, who thought that those who buy condom have illicit relationship and are suffering from STI or HIV/AIDS. To wipe out such negative connotation from the mindset of the common people, effort should be made to develop IEC materials and promote condom promotion programmes, safeguarding the cultural stigma. Proper planning is required to expand the usage of condom consistently and correctly.

## REFERENCES

Gujarat State AIDS Control Society (2005), *Annual Report* up to March 31, 2005. Ahmedabad: Gujarat State AIDS Control Society.

National AIDS Control Organisation. (2005) *India's Resolves to Defeat HIV/AIDS*. New Delhi: Ministry of Health and Family Welfare, Government of India.

(http://www.avert.org/aidsstigma.htm)

(http://www.developmentinaction.org/newspages/index/67.php)

Spring (1998), *Network: Men and Reproductive Health;* Vol. 18, No. 3.

Weller, S. and Davis, K. (2003), *Condom effectiveness in reducing heterosexual HIV transmission*. The Cochrane Library, Issue 2. Oxford: Update Software.

http://www.fhi.org/en/RH/Pubs/Network/v18_3/index.htm

# SECTION TWO

# Government Health Services

5

# Health Communication and Family Welfare Services in Madhya Pradesh

## An Overview and Future Challenges

*Md. Irfan Khan*

### Introduction

The paradigm shift in population policies from quantity to quality has been the growing concern for the policy-makers and programme managers since the induction of Reproductive and Child Health (RCH) programme was formally announced on April 1, 1996. This new RCH programme integrates all family welfare and women and child health services with the explicit objective of providing beneficiaries with need base, client centred, demand driven high quality integrated RCH services (MOH&FW, New Delhi, 1998). Under the RCH programme the State Government has been given directives to implement the programme under specific guidelines to achieve the desired health and demographic goals. In turn, like several other States, Government of Madhya Pradesh took various initiatives and has shown full commitment to implement the programme in order to achieve the desire goals by 2011. State initiatives across the country however, have not been uniform partly due to its existing operational difficulties with limited infrastructure and human resources in addition to financial constraints. The result of the paradigm shift across the States is not encouraging as the performance in several States have declined including that of Madhya Pradesh (Population Policy of Madhya Pradesh, 2000). It is, however, assumed that distinctly poor performing States will perpetuate its previous system of functioning for quite some time due to the momentum effect until they gain a certain level of acceleration from the new approach and programme inputs. Hence the fluctuation of performance in several States should not be seen as a setback to the programme but the momentum effect of previous service delivery system.

Madhya Pradesh is one among the several poor performing States now reaching close to many States of better performance, ensuring population stabilization and improvement in quality of life through implementing RCH programme in a comprehensive manner from the network of its existing health facilities*. Figure 5.1 provides the existing operational structure for health delivery system.

The Government of Madhya Pradesh has realized the seriousness of rapid growing population with high infant and child mortality rates. Therefore, the Government has decided to set the goal of achieving replacement fertility level of 2.1 by 2011. Looking ahead a change of current level of CPR from 22 to 65; IMR from 94 to 62; MMR from 498 per 100000 live birth to around 220 by 2011.

---

* The health services in rural areas of Madhya Pradesh are provided through the network of Health and Family Welfare delivery system. As on June 1997 an extensive network of 229 Community Health Centres (CHC), 1193 Primary Health Centres (PHC) and 8741 Sub-centres have been in operation to provide primary health-care at village level (Annual Report, 2000-2001).

Each Sub-centre is managed by one female and a male multipurpose health-worker covering a population of 5,000 in plain areas and 3,000 in hilly, tribal, backward and difficult terrains. Similarly, each primary health-centre is staffed with a Medical Officer, a Pharmacists, Staff Nurses, Female Multipurpose Health-Worker, Health-Educators, Laboratory Technician, Female Health Assistant, Male Health Assistant besides other four to five administrative staff. A PHC covers a population of 30,000 in the plain area and 20,000 in the hilly, tribal, backward and difficult terrain. Likewise each community health-centre is staffed with a medical, surgical, child specialist and a Gynaecologist each. In addition to 25 other paramedical and administrative staff, it has 30 indoor beds, well-equipped laboratories and X-ray facility. It covers approximately 80,000 to 1,20,000 rural population.

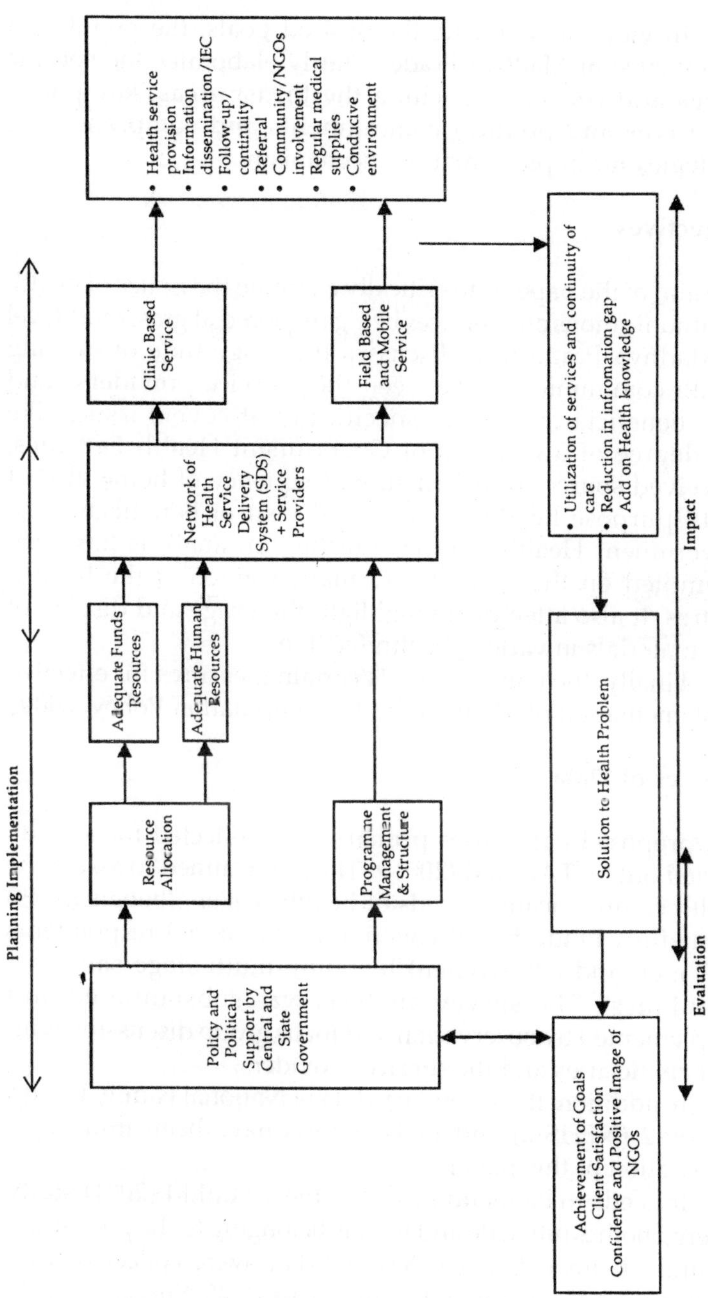


**Fig. 5.1: Operational Structure for Health Service Delivery System**

In view of achieving the desired goals, the population policy 2000 of Madhya Pradesh fairly elaborates the specific issues and concerns touching the thrust areas, key policy initiatives and political commitments and comprehensive strategies for implementation mechanism.

**Objectives**

The aim of the paper is to critically examine the issues of health communications and services being rendered at grassroots level in Madhya Pradesh. It discusses the magnitude of existing health communication between the "service providers" and the "beneficiaries". More specifically, it covers issues like the degree of awareness of Government Health Facilities, perceived sources of information, frequency of home visit of multi-purpose health-workers and visit of beneficiaries to Government Health Centres. Further, an analysis has been attempted on the type of information given at the health-centres. It also attempts to highlight the usage and display of IEC materials in various health facilities.

Finally, the paper suggests certain measures for effective implementation of Madhya Pradesh Population Policy, 2000.

**Sources of Data**

The proposed paper uses primary data collected for a study carried out by TALEEM (2001)[1]. The study aimed to assess the health communication needs of health seekers (beneficiaries) in Madhya Pradesh and covered a total of 969 respondents (343 men and 626 women) by using multi-stage sampling techniques[2]. The survey analysis was substantiated and supplemented by observation and focus group discussion with the beneficiaries and the service providers.

In addition, the secondary data of National Family Health Survey-2 (NFHS-2) and RCH reports have been utilised in preparation of this paper[3].

It needs to be mentioned that the TALEEM (2001) study covered both adult male and female belonging to the poor strata of rural Madhya Pradesh. NFHS-2 data were collected from "ever-married" women in the age group15-49. Similarly, RCH data were collected from currently married women in the age group 15-44 representing both rural and urban segments of population of the State. In this respect, the respondents and the reference period vary in three surveys depending upon the focus of these studies. Hence any direct comparison of the data particularly between TALEEM and NFHS or RCH survey may be misleading. However, it is assumed that NFHS-2 and RCH results would be more or less comparable because of the similar nature of the studies. Further, regardless of the differentials in the focus and methodology of these studies, all the three sets of data together are indicative of definitive trends of the prevailing situation in Madhya Pradesh.

## Results

### *Awareness about Government Health Facilities and Services*

In the present scenario, it is hard to set up and sustain health facilities in every village of Madhya Pradesh due to very high direct and indirect cost. However, this has been made up through the creation of network of Primary Health Centres (PHCs) and Sub-centres (SCs) that would meet the need of primary health-care at the peripheral level. In addition, the expansion and up-gradation of many sub-centres to PHCs and PHCs to referral units have augmented health services in the State. The TALEEM survey (2001) put forth the assessment of the awareness of the availability of health facilities within 10 km. radius from the respondents' villages. The TALEEM analysis reveals that 9 out of 10 respondents (87 per cent) were aware of the availability of the government health facilities within the radius of 10 kilometres from their villages. The analysis indicates that more males than females were aware of the availability of government health centres. Table 5.1 indicates that those who were aware of the availability of healthcare facilities also knew largely about the availability of basic health services such as immunization (79 per cent), malaria (68 per cent), antenatal/postnatal care (45 per cent), diarrhoea (40 per cent) and family planning (28 per cent). The level of awareness about these services was more or less same among both males and females. However, the awareness about other national healthcare programmes to combat communicable and other diseases like Tuberculosis, Leprosy, Blindness and HIV/AIDS was very low among them.

The other two surveys (NFHS-2 and RCH) do not provide such information. However TALEEM's study as indicated above suggests that information about the available services is not universal and the layer of information becomes thinner for all other national vertical disease control programmes causing deep concern.

**Table 5.1:** Awareness about the Availability of Government Health Facilities and Sources of Information

*(Percentage)*

| *Health Facilities* | *Male* | *Female* | *Total* |
|---|---|---|---|
| **Aware of Govt. Health Facilities within 10 km.** | 91.5 | 83.9 | 86.6 |
| **Total No. of Respondents** | **343** | **626** | **969** |
| **Awareness of Health Services*** | | | |
| ANC/PNC | 42.0 | 46.9 | 45.1 |
| Immunization | 80.9 | 77.7 | 78.9 |
| Diarrhoea | 36.9 | 41.7 | 39.9 |
| Pneumonia | 19.1 | 20.0 | 19.7 |
| Malaria | 71.3 | 65.9 | 67.9 |
| TB | 3.2 | 2.1 | 2.5 |
| Leprosy | 2.9 | 1.9 | 2.3 |
| Blindness | 3.5 | 1.1 | 2.0 |
| HIV/AIDS | 6.4 | 2.5 | 3.9 |
| Family Planning | 30.9 | 25.7 | 27.7 |
| Others | 25.8 | 28.4 | 27.4 |
| **Source of Information*** | | | |
| Self | 75.2 | 61.3 | 66.5 |
| Relative/Friends | 13.4 | 19.0 | 16.9 |
| Health-Worker/ANM | 17.8 | 20.0 | 19.2 |
| Member of Panchayat/Health Guide | 4.8 | 3.0 | 3.7 |
| Print Materials | 1.6 | 0.9 | 1.1 |
| Others | 5.4 | 11.2 | 9.1 |
| **No. of Respondents aware of Health Facilities** | **314** | **525** | **839** |

* Percentages based on those who are aware of Health Facilities.
*Source*: TALEEM-CNA, 2001.

**Source of Information about Health Facilities**

Table 5.1 indicates that 67 per cent respondents know about the location of existing health facilities in and around their villages through making self visit to health centres and hence did not mention any specific source(s) for obtaining this information. Two major sources of information however as reported were the health-workers (19 per cent) and relatives and friends (17 per cent). In Focus Group Discussions (FGDs) Aanganwadi Workers and Mahila Swasthya Sevika were mentioned as sources of information and in a few instances Sarpanch was also mentioned as a source of information.

**Home Visit of Health Workers and Service Delivery**

Multi Purpose Health Workers (MPHW) are expected to visit every household regularly in their assigned (catchment) areas. During house to house visit, multi-purpose health-worker-female, popularly known as ANM is required to monitor various aspect of health of women and children. The ANM is expected to provide information related to health and family planning, counsel and motivate women to adopt appropriate health and family planning practices and deliver and coordinate services for other healthcare programme. Similarly multi-purpose male health-workers are responsible for public health and sanitation work. They are also responsible for motivating men for family planning, distributing condoms, organizing camps and coordinating family planning work with the ANM. Though it was planned that both male and female health-workers would cover approximately the same areas and population, in practice the number of male MPHW is far less than the female MPHW or the ANM in the country and so in Madhya Pradesh also. As of March 1990, there were only 82,000 male MPHWs working in the programme as compared to 140,000 female MPHW in the whole of country (Srinivasan, K., 1995).

In order to examine the process of health-service delivery and health communication at village level, respondents were asked whether any health-workers have visited them during the last three months prior to the survey. Table 5.2 reveals that overall, 53 per cent of the respondents were contacted at home by male and female health-workers including the Aanganwadi workers. Further analysis indicates 38 per cent female health-workers (ANMs), 25 per cent male health-workers and 23 per cent Aanganwadi workers had home visited. The variations in response to the frequency of home visit by the health-workers between male and female respondents were observed though not so large. On the other hand most of the participants in Focus Group Discussions (FGDs) stated that the visit of ANM was not so frequent and generally ANMs intensify their frequency of visits during the polio vaccination drive.

**Table 5.2:** Home Visit of Health Workers in Last 3 Months

*(Percentage)*

| *Visit and Use of IEC Material* | *Male* | *Female* | *Total* |
|---|---|---|---|
| **Visited by** | | | |
| ANM / MPHW (F) | 37.6 | 37.7 | 37.7 |
| MPHW (M) | 24.2 | 25.1 | 24.8 |
| Anganwadi Worker | 23.9 | 22.5 | 23.0 |
| **Visited by any Health-Worker** | **53.6** | **52.2** | **52.7** |
| **Type of Information Given** | | | |
| Not visited by any Health-Worker | 46.4 | 47.8 | 47.3 |
| ANC/PNC | 14.3 | 18.1 | 16.7 |
| Immunization | 43.7 | 42.8 | 43.1 |
| Diarrhoea | 14.6 | 17.1 | 16.2 |
| Pneumonia | 4.7 | 7.8 | 6.7 |
| Malaria | 27.1 | 29.1 | 28.4 |
| TB | 0.9 | 1.9 | 1.5 |
| Leprosy | 3.8 | 1.9 | 2.6 |
| Blindness | 0.9 | 1.3 | 1.1 |
| HIV/AIDS | 3.5 | 2.6 | 2.9 |
| Family Planning | 20.4 | 16.9 | 18.2 |
| Others | 12.2 | 10.9 | 11.4 |
| **Total No. of Respondents** | **343** | **626** | **969** |

*Source*: TALEEM-CNA, 2001.

While visiting the individual homes, these workers imparted information on various health issues. They discussed mainly about Immunization (43 per cent), Malaria (28 per cent), family planning (18 per cent), antenatal/postnatal care (17 per cent) and diarrhoea (16 per cent). Less than two per cent of the respondents indicated that they ever discussed about the Tuberculosis, Leprosy, Blindness and HIV/AIDS. This could possibly be the main reason why respondents are not aware of other services for several communicable and non-communicable diseases at different health facilities. However, FGDs with community members reveal that there has been a common opinion that community and group meetings or house-to-house visit by the health-workers would provide an ample opportunity to interact with and acquired health-related information from them.

According to NFHS-2 report, overall only 9 per cent of the women in M.P. (10 per cent in rural and 6 per cent in urban areas) have been visited by Government and/or private health-workers at home during past 12 months preceding the survey. The report also mentions that these women, on average received two home visits during the past 12 months. Further, it suggested that among those who were visited at least once, the main purpose of home visit was for immunization services (41 per cent). The other health matters discussed included treatment of health problems (35 per cent), family planning (27 per cent), child-care (23 per cent) and antenatal care (10 per cent). As expected most of the pregnant women and women with children age three years discussed immunization as compared to other issues. RCH (1998-99) report gives almost comparable figures of ANN/LHV visits (11 per cent as against 10 per cent in NFHS).

Madhya Pradesh has been ranked 12th among 32 States and Union Territories in matters of health-worker's visit. This clearly reveals that the purpose of making home visit by MPHW has been diminishing. The meagre frequency of health-worker's visit could be due to several reasons like shortage of the required number of health-workers, inaccessibility and transportation problem. Lack of worker's motivation and negligence towards their job performance however, cannot be overlooked. This is where the programme has to evolve a viable and effective mechanism to improve the services at peripheral level. The State has already initiated the steps for involving all stakeholders, particularly the Panchayati Raj Institutions, urban local bodies, the NGOs, Jan Swasth Rakshak, Mahila Swasth Sangh, Mahila Mandal and Youths for community mobilization and participation in the family welfare programme.

**Visit to Government Health Centre**

Figure 5.2 indicates that 37 per cent of the respondents had opportunity to visit the government health facilities for curative purpose during the last three months prior to the survey. During these visits as indicated in Table 5.3 they were also given health-related information apart from the treatment/advice sought for. Though it was mostly centred around immunization (45 per cent), malaria (44 per cent), family planning (33 per cent), diarrhoea (28 per cent) and breast-feeding (25 per cent). Communication on immunization and malaria was much higher than other health problems.

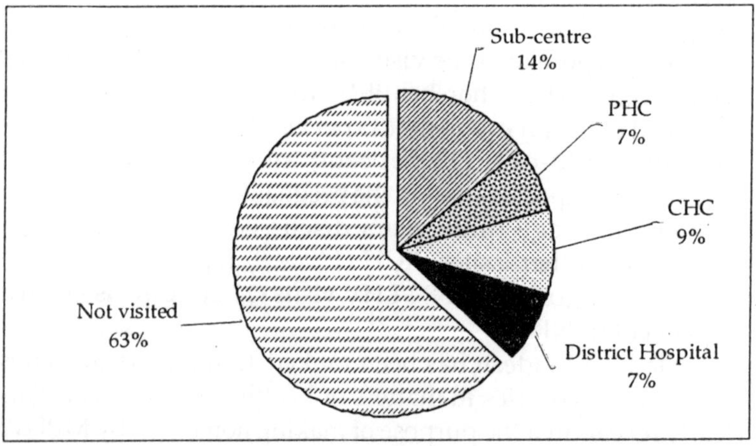


**Fig. 5.2:** Visit to Government Health Facilities in Last Three Months

This is an indication that communication does take place between health providers and the patients during visit to the health centres also.

The NFHS report indicated that the matters discussed during the visit to health facilities were largely confined to the treatment (59 per cent) or for a childcare (50 per cent), immunization (16 per cent) and ANC (8 per cent). A negligible percentage (i.e. less than 2 per cent) of the women reported about the discussions held on other health issues like family planning, breastfeeding, nutrition, disease prevention, oral re-hydration and sanitation. The NFHS highlights the lack of integration of health and family planning services in Madhya Pradesh.

**Table 5.3:** Type of Health Information Given at the Government Health Centres

*(Percentage)*

| *Type of Information Given* | *Male* | *Female* | *Total* |
|---|---|---|---|
| Breast Feeding | 19.4 | 28.7 | 25.2 |
| Immunization | 45.5 | 45.3 | 45.4 |
| Diarrhoea | 29.1 | 26.5 | 27.5 |
| Pneumonia | 13.4 | 16.6 | 15.4 |
| Malaria | 39.6 | 46.2 | 43.7 |
| Leprosy | 9.7 | 7.2 | 8.1 |
| Blindness | 4.5 | 4.0 | 4.2 |
| HIV/AIDS | 12.7 | 6.7 | 9.0 |
| Family Planning | 35.8 | 30.5 | 32.5 |
| Others | 11.9 | 13.9 | 13.2 |
| **No. of Respondents visited Health Centres** | **134** | **223** | **357** |

*Source*: TALEEM-CNA, 2001.

Similarly, RCH report has indicated that only 30 per cent of the women had visited government health facilities during the last three months. Rank-wise position of Madhya Pradesh in health-care services is, 23rd among 32 States and Union Territories indicating a low utilization of the health services.

## Exposure to IEC Materials

Health facilities also act as the sources of information through the exhibits and displays of IEC materials within the premises. Table 5.4 shows that the people while visiting the health facilities had a chance to look at the IEC material displayed. Overall 63 per cent of the respondents reported to have seen IEC material displayed at various health facilities.

**Table 5.4:** Display of IEC Material at the Health Centres

*(Percentage)*

| *Display of IEC Materials* | *Male* | *Female* | *Total* |
|---|---|---|---|
| **Display of IEC Material at:** | | | |
| Sub-centre | 23.1 | 25.1 | 24.4 |
| PHC | 12.7 | 13.9 | 13.4 |
| CHC | 19.4 | 14.8 | 16.5 |
| Hospital | 17.9 | 8.5 | 12.0 |
| Any of the above | 69.4 | 58.7 | 62.7 |
| **Type of IEC Material Seen During the Visit** | | | |
| Not seen | 30.6 | 41.3 | 37.3 |
| ANC/PNC | 26.1 | 19.3 | 21.8 |
| Immunization | 59.0 | 0.2 | 51.0 |
| Diarrhoea | 11.2 | 13.9 | 12.9 |
| Pneumonia | 6.0 | 11.7 | 9.5 |
| Malaria | 25.4 | 26.0 | 25.8 |
| TB | 6.0 | 2.7 | 3.9 |
| Leprosy | 14.2 | 9.9 | 11.5 |
| Blindness | 3.0 | 1.3 | 2.0 |
| HIV/AIDS | 25.4 | 7.6 | 14.3 |
| Family Planning | 35.8 | 22.0 | 27.2 |
| Others | 6.0 | 4.5 | 5.0 |
| **Received IEC Material** | **13.4** | **15.2** | **14.6** |
| **Total No. of Respondents visited Health Centre in last 3 months** | **134** | **223** | **357** |

*Source*: TALEEM-CNA, 2001.

Facility-wise breakup indicates that 24 per cent of the respondents have seen IEC materials displayed at the Sub-centre followed by 17 per cent at CHCs. Thirteen per cent of them reported that they had seen the IEC display in PHC and 12 per cent of them have mentioned district hospital also.

Of the 63 per cent who were exposed to IEC material during their visit to any of the government health facilities, 51 per cent of them have seen IEC material displayed on immunization. Another 27 per cent of them had seen IEC displys on family planning; 26 per cent on malaria and 22 per cent on antenatal/postnatal care. In FGD too, very few who were literate, mentioned that they had seen pamphlets on

Leprosy, TB, HIV/AIDS and Polio while visiting PHCs and SCs. IEC materials are available at various government health facilities. However, it was pointed out that none of the health functionaries bothered to explain the IEC material.

The survey data also indicated the minimal use of IEC materials by the ANM during home visit as only 13 per cent of the women confirmed that ANM had made use of IEC materials during the discussion on health and family welfare matters (Fig. 5.3). The participants of the focus group discussions firmly believed that IEC material could be more useful if the health worker bothered to explain to them.

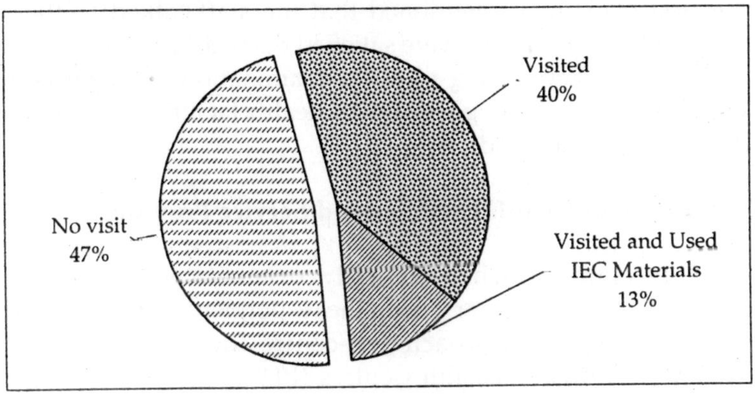


**Fig. 5.3:** Usage of IEC Material during Home Visit by Health-Workers

Some of the participants of FGD mentioned that they have seen posters on the walls of Panchayats and school buildings also. However, they could not understand and read the messages because of their illiteracy. They understood the messages only when someone happened to explain to them.

## Quality of Care and Satisfaction

Certain parameters of quality of health care have been examined in NFHS-2 and RCH surveys in order to understand the quality of services rendered to the benificiaries. Both the surveys have revealed almost identical results on the level of satisfaction. Overall, about 90 per cent of the rural women who were visited by the health-workers indicated satisfaction over the amount of time the health-workers spent with them. However, this parameter should not be seen in isolation as far as the rural women are concerned who are already deprived of basic health services. They have little expectation from the service providers. Hence, even occasional visit of the health-worker could lead to a high appreciation of services. The NFHS survey suggests that by and large most of the women were satisfied with the amount of time spent with them by the health worker and considered sufficient (91 per cent). Ninety-six per cent of women mentioned that the staff talked to them nicely while 68 per cent were satisfied that staff respected their need for privacy during physical examination. In regards to the cleanliness of the government health facilities, almost all of them were satisfied.

**Preference of Health Facilities and Service Provider**

The Sub-centres, which theoretically cover outreach population could attract, only 21 per cent of the respondents who reported that they would approach sub-centre for the purpose of treatment. Primary Health Centres (PHCs) and Community Health Centres (CHCs) were preferred by 13 per cent and 19 per cent of the respondents respectively (Fig. 5.4). The preference for the private doctor/clinics was as high as 34 per cent.

The first preference for getting treatment is again the private doctors (44 per cent) followed by the government doctors (40 per cent, Fig. 5.5) and health-workers are their secondary preference. Hence, utilization of the sub-centres seemed to be limited for specific services. Focus Group Discussions clearly revealed that the utilization of sub-centres was low in spite of the fact that these facilities were available close to the residence. The preference for CHCs and district hospitals has been mainly because people have more confidence in doctors who are normally available at CHCs and hospitals rather than at PHCs and sub-centres. These facilities are approached for the treatment of both minor and major ailments while sub-centres are mostly availed for vaccination services.

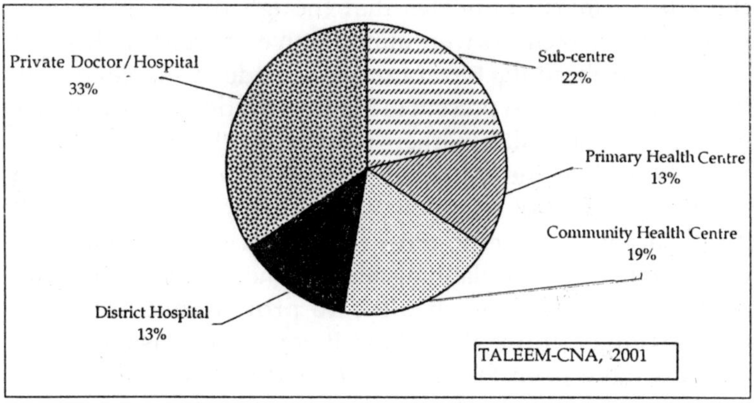


**Fig. 5.4:** Preference for Health Facilities

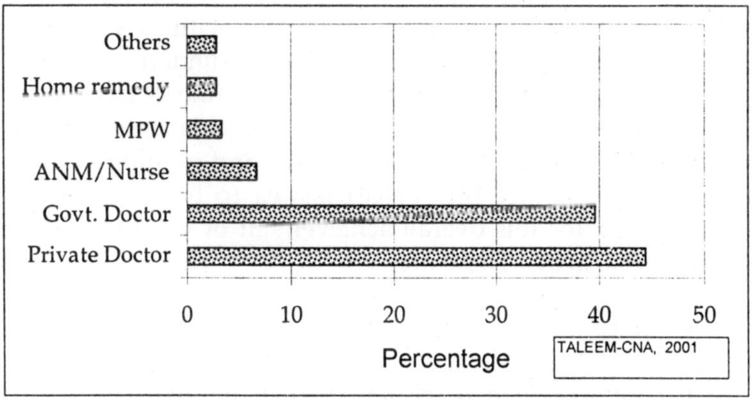


**Fig. 5.5:** Preference for Service Providers

## Conclusion and Recommendations

Keeping in view the previous experiences of programme formulation and implementation and research and evaluation, the State policy has to look into the thrust areas carefully. The programme implementation must be carried out in an integrated manner under the on-going RCH programme. This paper brings out certain critical health issues and draws the attention to the programme managers and service providers. The study clearly indicates that though the awareness of existing health facilities were almost universal, the beneficiaries are not sure about the type of services made available to meet their unmet needs. At present in Madhya Pradesh the frequency of home visit of health-workers is far below the required level. At the same time, the utilization of existing Government health facilities is poor but relatively better among the poor section of the society. Currently, most of the services are limited to immunization, family planning and to some extent the childcare leaving aside the other healthcare programmes. The IEC activities either during the field visit or patient's visit to health facilities have been taken lightheartedly. The government health facilities have not come up with the level of people's expectation and hence they still prefer to go to private doctor or hospital despite financial constraints leading under utilization of existing government health facilities. It is thus essential for the concerned State machinery to undertake certain corrective measures if at all the health programmes have to go a long way in order to achieve the desired goals. Based on the results of three studies discussed above and existing known problems, there are few broad issues to be taken in to consideration for this overall achievement of the health and demographic goals. These are:

- There is need to have required number health staff including medical officer.
- Re-enforcement of the defined roles and responsibilities of all categories of health staff be executed.
- The programme must evolve appropriate mechanism to enhance the frequency of home visit by the health-workers for service delivery and follow-up of Maternal and Child Health and Family Planning services.
- A viable mechanism need to be elaborated for involving all stakeholders in the delivery of reproductive and child health services.
- Periodic skill up-gradation programme for various categories of health personnel should be made part and

parcel of the programme implementation. Orientation to field staff be given on quality aspects of health services.

- The processes of appropriate IEC dissemination mechanism from top (Centre/State) to bottom (individual/village) need to be strengthened.
- Continuous supervision and monitoring of service delivery mechanism at the grassroots level be ascertained.
- Timely supply of medicine, vaccines, contraceptives and IEC material be assured.
- Elected Panchayat and Nagarpalika members need to be solidly grounded in understanding and addressing community and women's health needs as part of their responsibility.
- Internal assessment and operations research be carried out repeatedly in order to get the continuous feedback for future course of action and improvement.

*Acknowledgements*

The author gratefully acknowledges Dr. Binod C. Agrawal, Director and Professor J.K. Doshi of TALEEM for their encouragement and valuable suggestions in preparing this paper. The author is also indebted to Dr. Mitali Chakraborty for her suggestions and to Mr. Vijay Uttekar for typing and graphic presentation of this paper.

## NOTES

1. For details *see* report on "Communication Need Assessment" in Madhya Pradesh. The study was carried out on behalf of Public Health and Family Welfare Department, Government of Madhya Pradesh under DANIDA supported MP-Basic Health Services Programme, Phase-III. The document (unpublished) was submitted to the State Health and Family Welfare Department in September 2001.
2. In the multistage sampling, at the first stage of sampling, six districts representing six geo-cultural zones of the State were selected. In

each district two PHCs (one better performing and another poor performing) were selected which constituted the second stage of the sampling. At the third stage, one sub-centre village and another remote village were selected from each of the selected PHC. Thus in each district, four villages were selected and from each village 40 households belonging to the poor strata (according to the villagers perception) of the selected village were again randomly selected. In each of the household only one adult respondent preferably the senior most person, either male or female were interviewed as per the agreed design of the study. The data were collected between May-July 2001.

3. NFHS-2 survey was held in 1998-99, covering 6749 households and 6941 ever-married women age 15-49 in the whole of Madhya Pradesh while RCH survey was carried out in two phases between 1998-99, covering 46355 households and 41250 eligible women in all 45 districts of M.P.

## REFERENCES

*Annual Report* (2000-2001), Department of Public Health and Family Welfare, Government of Madhya Pradesh.

Anrudh K. Jain (ed.) (1992), *Managing Quality of Care in Population Programme*, Kumarian Press, USA, Inc., 630.

International Institute of Population Sciences, Mumbai, 1998-1999. Reproductive and Child Health—Rapid Household Survey Phase I and II, India Report.

Ministry of Health and Family Welfare (1998), *Manual in Community Needs Assessment Approach in Family Welfare Programme*, Department of Family Welfare, Ministry of Health and Family Welfare, Government of India

National Family Health Survey-2 (1998-99), Madhya Pradesh Report, International Institute of Population Sciences, Mumbai.

*Population Policy of Madhya Pradesh* (2000), Department of Health and Family Welfare, Government of Madhya Pradesh.

Srinivasan K. (1995), *Regulating Reproduction in India's Population—Efforts, Results and Recommendations*, Sage Publication, New Delhi.

TALEEM Research Foundation, (2001), *Communication Needs Assessment*, DANIDA supported MPBHS Programme Phase-III and Department of PH&FW, Government of Madhya Pradesh.

# 6

# Perception about Government Health Services in Maharashtra
## A Sociological Analysis

*Md. Irfan Khan* and *Binod C. Agrawal*

### Introduction

The Government of India is committed to provide "Health for All" through the primary health care approach. The mission got a further boost when India became a signatory of the International Conference on Population and Development (ICPD) declaration in 1994. The declaration focused on meeting reproductive health needs involving a range of quality health services. Reproductive and Child Health (RCH) intervention initiated in 1996 in India has been a step further in translating the ICPD action programme. The RCH programme unifies the components of Child Survival and Safe Motherhood (CSSM) programme with the components of Sexually Transmitted Diseases (STD) and Reproductive Tract Infections (RTI). The RCH programme is expected to deliver need-based, client-oriented and demand driven high quality integrated RCH services (Ministry of Health and Family Welfare, 1998).

The new paradigm incorporates a comprehensive reproductive health programme making a shift from target-oriented (quantity) to target-free approach (quality) according to the manual on Community Needs Assessment Approach, Ministry of Health and Family Welfare, Government of India. Some of the essential components of programme strategy included were community participation in planning for services, up-gradation of health facilities and multi-sector coordination for implementation and monitoring of services. Interaction between patients and health providers and patients satisfaction from their services have been extensively focused at the grassroots level; not only to boost the image of the health services, but also to ensure the optimum use of health services.

The World Bank supported State Health Systems Development Projects have undertaken the task of institutional development and quality improvement in health services in their respective States. It is believed that better quality health services improve the level of patient's satisfaction and utilization of health services (Jain, 1992; Bruce, 1990).

## Objectives

The paper broadly examines a commonman's perception about the existing government health facilities, service providers and the level of patients' satisfaction in the State of Maharashtra.

The paper attempts to analyse accessibility, infrastructure, human power, stock and supply and health workers' interaction with the community. Also perception of people about service providers' behaviour and the level of patients' satisfaction have been analysed. The paper is expected to provide some insights into the overall quality of health services in Maharashtra and would pinpoint the shortfalls within the health system affecting the desired quality of services.

## Sources of Data

The paper is based on the analyses of data collected in three recent Maharashtra health surveys.

1. ***Reproductive and Child Health Project—Rapid Household Survey, 2002*[1]:** The main aim of the RCH survey was to collect information at the district level on reproductive and child healthcare indicators, in order to strengthen decentralized planning and implementation of the programme. The survey was conducted in the year 2002 in the States of Maharashtra. The survey covered 18 districts (50 per cent) of the districts of the State.

2. ***Facility Survey under Reproductive and Child Health Project, 1999*:** The primary objective of the facility survey was to assess the existing situation of the healthcare facilities available in the government health care establishments at different levels (Facility Survey, 1999). The survey was carried out in 1999 in 13 districts of Maharashtra. The survey covered 10 district hospitals, 50 First Referral Units (FRUs), 71 Community Health Centres (CHCs) and 645 Primary Health Centres (PHCs).

3. ***Satisfaction Assessment of Patients and Health Providers, 2002*[2]:** The aim of the study was to assess the follow up effect of Maharashtra Health Service Development Project (MHSDP) on State Health System for quality services. The study involved exit survey of 1341 indoor and outdoor patients. It also covered 31 FGDs, 56 case studies and observation of 165 outpatients apart from collecting profile of 32 hospitals/CHCs spread across 8 districts of the State. In case of Health service providers, 138 doctors, 154 nurses, 120 laboratory technicians 138 administrative staff and 169 Class-IV staff were interviewed.

## Analysis

Three surveys carried out at different points in time having somewhat related objectives have been analysed to draw major conclusions.

### *Strength of Government Health Facilities*

Primary Health Centres (PHCs) is expected to provide both preventive and curative health and family welfare services. It includes delivery of RCH services like antenatal care and immunization. In addition, in-patients and out-patients services are also provided. Primary health centres normally serve a population of approximately 30,000 in the plain areas and 20,000 in the Hilly/Tribal areas. It acts as referral units for six sub-centres that act as contact points between PHC and the community. A PHC is expected to have a medical officer and altogether 14 paramedical and other support staff. It should have 4-6 beds for the patients. The strength of a PHC lies broadly in its basic infrastructural facilities like a self owned building, toilet, continuous supply of water, electricity, labour room, laboratory, telephone, functional vehicles and beds for in-patients (IIPS, 2001)[3]. The facility survey in Maharashtra covered 645 PHCs. For the purpose of analysis, adequacy of four components like infrastructure, staff, medical supply and equipments have been considered. If any component has at least 60 per cent of all the critical items included, it is taken as adequately equipped. Maharashtra State analysis shows that 88 per cent of the PHCs infrastructure is adequately equipped against 36 per cent for the country as a whole. Similarly, 60 per cent of PHCs have adequate number of staff for service delivery, while it is 38 per cent for the country. The supply of basic drugs and contraceptives and basic equipments necessary for service delivery is reported to be much better in the State as compared to the national average (87% against 31% for supply and 96% against 56% for the country) (Table 6.1).

**Table 6.1:** Availability of Maharashtra Health Facilities

| *Type of Facility* | *Total Number* | *Adequately Equipped (in percentages)* | | | |
|---|---|---|---|---|---|
| | | *Infrastructure* | *Staff* | *Supply* | *Equipment* |
| District Hospital | 10 | 90.0 (94.0) | 80.0 (84.0) | 20.0 (26.0) | 100 (89.0) |
| FRU | 50 | 100 (84.0) | 34.0 (46.0) | 50.0 (26.0) | 34.0 (69.0) |
| CHC | 71 | 97.0 (66.0) | 28.0 (25.0) | 8.0 (10.0) | 10.0 (49.0) |
| PHC | 645 | 88.0 (36.0) | 60.0 (38.0) | 87.0 (31.0) | 96.0 (56.0) |

*Note*: Figures in parentheses are national average.
*Source*: Facility Survey under RCH Project, IIPS, Mumbai, 1999.

On the whole, the analysis indicated better infrastructure of health facilities in Maharashtra in comparison to the national scenario. Relatively PHCs are far better in Maharashtra in terms of the critical inputs as compared to the national average. However, the State lags behind the national average in the areas of human power, supply and equipment particularly in FRUs, CHCs and district hospital.

### *Accessibility of Health Facilities*

*(a) Location of Health Facilities*: The utilization of health services also depends upon the access to the physical location of the health facilities. It is in this context that RCH survey has made an attempt to understand how women perceive the convenience of location of the existing health facilities. The women who had visited government health facilities in last three months prior to the survey were asked a series of questions related to the health facilities and service providers. When they were asked about the convenience of location, more than three-fourth (77%) indicated that facilities are conveniently located (Fig. 6.1). For the rest, it seems that access to the location is inconvenient.

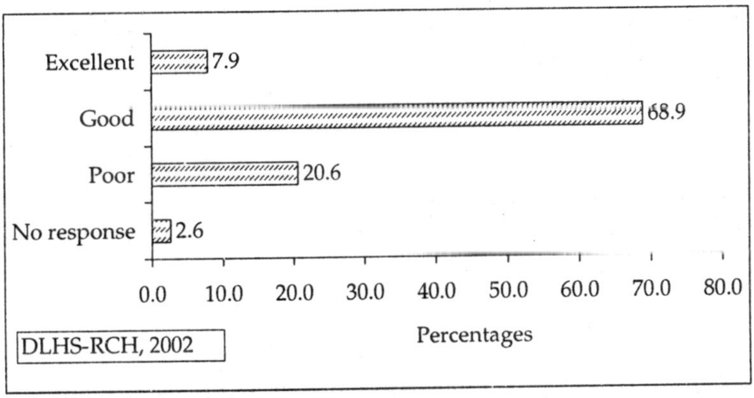


**Fig. 6.1:** Convenience of Health Facility Location

*(b) Health Service at Home*: In the rural areas, multipurpose health-workers are deputed to visit each household in their catchment areas to provide basic health care services to the community. During house-to-house visit, multi purpose female health-worker, popularly known as ANM is required to monitor various aspects of health of women and children. The ANM is expected to provide information related to health and family planning, counsel and motivate women to adopt

appropriate health and family planning practices and deliver and coordinate services for other healthcare programmes. Similarly, multi-purpose male health-workers are responsible for public health and sanitation work. They are also responsible for motivating men into family planning, distributing condoms, organizing camps and coordinating family planning work with the ANM. Though it was planned that both male and female health-workers would cover approximately the same areas and population, in practice the number of male MPHW is far less than the female MPHW or the ANM in the country. It is evident from the fact that as of March 1990, there were only 82,000 male MPHWs working in the programme as compared to 140,000 female MPHW in the whole of country (Srinivasan, 1995).

He survey revealed that only 12 per cent of the women reported that a health-worker has visited them during last three months prior to survey (Fig. 6.2). The meagre frequency of health worker's visit is largely due to the shortage of required number of health workers. Inaccessibility and lack of transportation are the other causes of low mobility of health-workers especially in rural areas. Also lack of workers' motivations and negligence towards their job cannot be overlooked (Khan, 2003). These are the areas where the programme has to evolve a viable and affective mechanism to improve the services at the peripheral level.

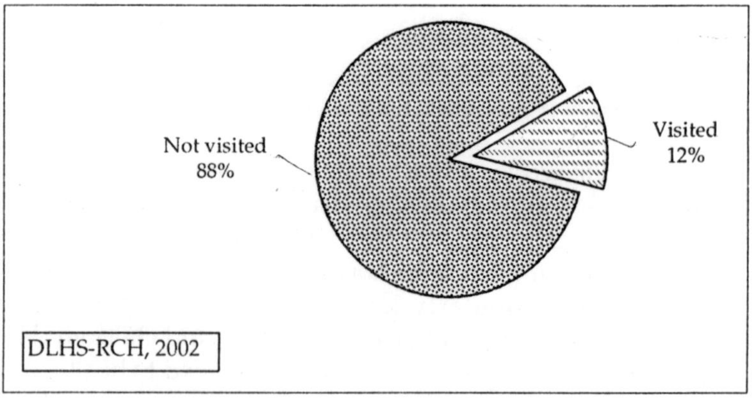


**Fig. 6.2:** Visit of Health-Worker in Last 3 Months

### *Operational Environment*

*(a) Waiting time*: Waiting time to see a doctor is another dimension of quality services. The length of waiting time depends on the daily turn over of patients and availability of required number of service providers (doctors). The satisfaction study revealed that on an average the patient had to wait for about nine minutes for getting the registration done. The average time taken for the registration was little higher for the indoor patients (11.3 minutes) than the outdoor patients (8.1 minutes) (Table 6.2).

**Table 6.2:** Mean Waiting Time by In-door and Out-door Patient

*(In minutes)*

| *Time Spent on Various Activities* | *Type of Patient* | | *Total* |
|---|---|---|---|
| | *Outdoor* | *Indoor* | |
| **Registration** | | | |
| Mean* | 8.1 | 11.3 | 8.5 |
| Number | 1109 | 160 | 1269 |
| **Doctor's Call** | | | |
| Mean* | 16.4 | 38.7 | 19.3 |
| Number | 1114 | 164 | 1278 |
| **Doctor's Consultation** | | | |
| Mean* | 5.9 | 8.6 | 6.2 |
| Number | 1117 | 172 | 1289 |
| **Medicine Counter** | | | |
| Mean* | 8.7 | 6.3 | 8.5 |
| Number | 971 | 103 | 1074 |

* Mean is calculated after excluding the missing cases.
*Source*: Satisfaction Assessment of Patient and Health Providers in the State of Maharashtra, 2002.

The average waiting time for the doctor's call for patients was 19.3 minutes (38.7 minutes for indoor and 16.4 minutes for outdoor). The doctor spent about 6.2 minutes of time with the patients (8.6 minutes for indoor and 5.9 minutes for outdoor). Similarly, on an average 8.5 minutes waiting time was mentioned for collecting the prescribed drugs. This was less for indoor (6.3 minutes) than the outdoor patients (8.7 minutes).

The RCH survey also provide a similar observation on the length of waiting time at the health facilities. Of the women who visited health facilities, around one-fourth have indicated that it took longer time to get the services. The 'average' and 'short time' spent for getting services were mentioned by 66 per cent and 5 per cent of the women respectively (Fig. 6.3).

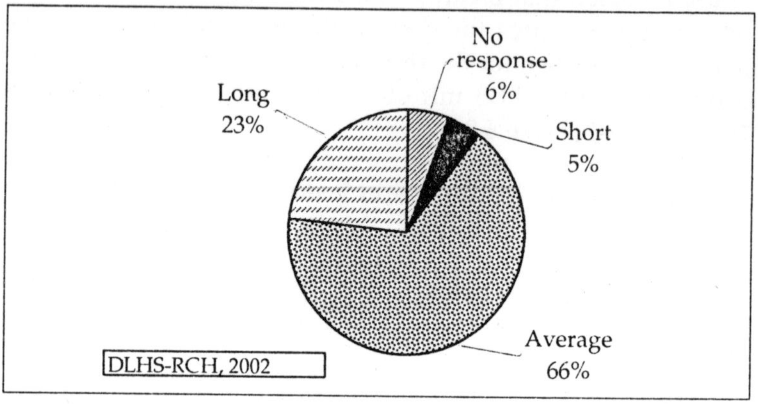


**Fig. 6.3:** Waiting Time

*(b)Attitude of Health Providers*: It is considered that the positive behaviour towards the client is an important component of quality services. The patients' satisfaction depends on how the service providers interact with them. It is in this context that women were asked to rate the health personnel as poor, good and excellent for their personal qualities like courtesy, respect and friendliness. By and large the personal manner of the doctors, nurses and other support staff were rated as 'good' (Fig. 6.4).

The satisfaction assessment study also gives a somewhat similar picture of the attitude of service providers. The study revealed that the attitude of staff at registration counter towards the patients was 'nice and helpful' (57%) and 'alright' (40%). Around 50 per cent of the patients (65% indoor and 47% outdoor) revealed the attitude of nurses as `kind' and another 21 per cent indicated 'very hard working'. However, the attitude of laboratory technicians and ward boys was mentioned 'nice and helpful' by 25-36 per cent of the patients (Table 6.3).

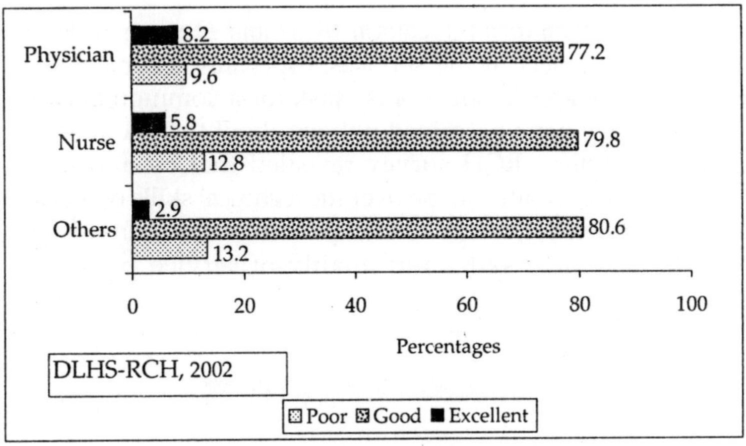


**Fig. 6.4:** Attitude of Health Providers

**Table 6.3:** Attitude of Staff Towards the Patients

| *Attitude* | *Type of Patient* | | *Total* |
|---|---|---|---|
| | *Outdoor* | *Indoor* | |
| **Attitude of Registration Staff** | | | |
| Nice and Helpful | 56.2 | 58.4 | 56.5 |
| Alright | 40.1 | 39.5 | 40.3 |
| Rude and indifferent | 3.6 | 2.2 | 3.4 |
| **Attitude of Nurse** | | | |
| Kind | 47.4 | 64.9 | 49.8 |
| Rude | 8.7 | 11.4 | 9.0 |
| Hardworking | 19.0 | 36.2 | 21.4 |
| Corrupt and inefficient | 4.2 | 5.4 | 4.3 |
| No response | 33.6 | 9.2 | 30.2 |
| **Attitude of Lab. Technician** | | | |
| Kind | 24.9 | 35.1 | 26.3 |
| Rude | 2.9 | 1.1 | 2.7 |
| Hardworking | 12.0 | 20.0 | 13.1 |
| No response | 65.9 | 50.2 | 63.8 |
| **Attitude of Ward Boy/Ayah** | | | |
| Nice and Helpful | 40.0 | 33.9 | 35.0 |
| No response | 60.0 | 66.1 | 65.0 |
| **Total Number of Patients** | **1156** | **185** | **1341** |

*Source*: Satisfaction Assessment of Patient and Health Providers in the State of Maharashtra, 2002

*(c) Perception about Technical Skills and Quality*: Judging the technical aspect of the services, especially technical skill of service provider is not an easy task for a common person. However, they have perceived notions about the goodness of service providers. RCH survey revealed that by and large women expressed satisfaction over the technical skills of service providers. However, nearly 10 to 13 per cent seemed unsatisfied over the technical skills and quality of service providers (Fig. 6.5).

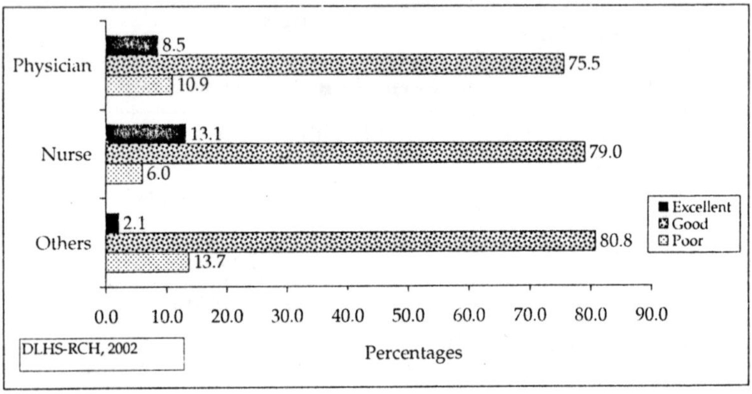


**Fig. 6.5:** Perception about Technical Skills and Quality

## *Satisfaction with Facilities and Treatment*

(a) Patient satisfaction undoubtedly has been a reflection of the impact of health services. The satisfaction study indicates that the degree of satisfaction with the existing medical facilities in the district hospital, sub-divisional hospital and community health centres is quite high (nearly 48% patients being fully satisfied and another 40% satisfied to some extent). Only 12 per cent of them said that they were not satisfied with the existing medical facilities. The level of satisfaction was witnessed more among the indoor patients (57%) than the outdoor patients (46%).

(b) Just as the patients were satisfied with the medical facilities they were also satisfied with the treatment. About half of the patients were fully satisfied with the doctors and the treatment; while another 36 per cent were satisfied to some extent. Only 30 per cent of the patients had shown dissatisfaction over the treatment. Again, more indoor patients (62%) than outdoor patients (48%) were fully satisfied with the treatment given by the doctors (Table 6.4).

**Table 6.4:** Satisfaction with Medical Facility and Doctors Treatment

| *Satisfaction Level* | *Type of Patient* | | *Total* |
|---|---|---|---|
| | *Outdoor* | *Indoor* | |
| **Medical Facility** | | | |
| Fully Satisfied | 46.2 | 56.8 | 47.7 |
| To some extend | 40.6 | 36.2 | 40.0 |
| Not satisfied/Cannot say | 13.2 | 7.0 | 12.4 |
| **Doctors Treatments** | | | |
| Fully Satisfied | 48.4 | 62.2 | 50.3 |
| To some extent | 37.6 | 28.6 | 36.4 |
| Not satisfied/Cannot say | 14.1 | 9.1 | 13.4 |
| **Total Number of Patients** | **1156** | **185** | **1341** |

*Source*: Satisfaction Assessment of Patient and Health Providers in the State of Maharashtra, 2002.

## Conclusion and Recommendation

Three surveys undoubtedly indicated a positive picture of Maharashtra health services and peoples' satisfaction from them. Three points clearly emerged. Firstly, the Governments continued efforts in improving the health services at PHC level have been well established and appreciated. Secondly, services seemed to have been made available in a friendly environment and patients seemed satisfied with the facilities and the health providers, including doctors. Thirdly, care and services did not vary much between indoor and outdoor patients. On the whole, it indicated a positive sign for the efforts put in, in meeting the health needs of the people.

The overall observations however, pinpointed two broad areas of concern to have effective and quality health services in the State. The peripheral coverage by the MPHW was limited and it needed to be strengthened in order to have better and direct communication between the health providers and the community at large. Without this linkage the educational, promotional and preventive activities would certainly be hampered. The other area of concern is the human power. It was observed that the required number of health providers, especially the doctors and nurses were not available according to the requirement, particularly in FRUs and CHCs. Priority has to be given for the deployment of health providers at FRUs and CHC level health facility. Adequate supply and equipments at FRUs/CHCs need to be improved and upgraded to treat the referral patients, who largely come from the rural areas.

### *Acknowledgements*

The authors gratefully acknowledge the valuable assistance of Shri Vijay Uttekar, who carried out the analysis, prepared power point presentation and graphics and also due thanks to Ms. Shalini Raghaviah for editorial assistance.

## NOTES

1. We are most grateful to International Institute for Population Sciences (IIPS), Mumbai which co-ordinated this national level survey as Nodal Agency and provided us the total data for further analysis. Please refer DLHS-RCH reports of IIPS, Mumbai for more details.
2. We are grateful to Maharashtra Health Service Development (MHSDP) Project officials for giving us the opportunity to carry out this survey and to incorporate part of the information in this paper.
3. The other strength is its manpower like medical officer, multipurpose health-worker (male and female), laboratory technician and support staff. Similarly, its supply of contraceptives, vaccines, medicines and IUD insertion kit, normal delivery kit, prophylactic drugs such as IFA and ORS is made regular. Its equipment like those essential for delivery, weighing machine, vaccine carrier, deep freezer and steam sterilizer drum, autoclave, labour room table are also made available.

## REFERENCES

Anrudh K. Jain (ed.) (1992), *Managing Quality of Care in Population Programme*, Kumarian Press, USA, Inc., 630.

Bruce, Judith (1990), Fundamental Elements of the Quality of Care: A Simple Framework. *Studies in Family Planning* 21,2:61-91.

IIPS, Mumbai, (2001), *Facility Survey-India, under Reproductive and Child Health Project*, Phase-I, 1999

Khan M.I. (2003), *Health Communication and Family Welfare Services in Madhya Pradesh—An Overview and Future Challenges*—Paper presented in the seminar on Population of Madhya Paradesh, Organized by Population Resource Centre, Bhopal on January 23-25, 2003.

Ministry of Health and Family Welfare (MoH&FW), (1998), *Manual on Community Needs Assessment Approach in Family Welfare Programme*, Department of Family Welfare, Government of India, New Delhi

Srinivasan, K. (1995), *Regulating Reproduction in India's Population—Efforts, Results and Recommendation*, Sage Publication, New Delhi.

TALEEM Research Foundation (2002), *Satisfaction Assessment of Patients and Health Providers in the State of Maharashtra*, MHSDP, Government of Maharashtra.

*SECTION THREE*

# Population, Tribal Health and Corporal Punishment

# 7

# Status of Safe Motherhood Programme in Madhya Pradesh

## Results From Health and Family Welfare Surveys

*Md. Irfan Khan* and *Mitali Chakarabarty*

### Introduction

Safe motherhood refers to all women receiving the care needed to be safe and healthy through pregnancy and childbirth. At the beginning of the Eighth Five Year Plan, India's Maternal and Child Health (MCH) programmes expanded vastly, integrating several other health programmes like Universal Immunization Programme (UIP), Oral Rehydration Therapy (ORT), aiming at improving the health of the mother and young children by providing them with facilities for prevention and treatment of major diseases. Even though these programmes did have a positive impact, the separate identity of each programme was creating problems in its effective management. Therefore, Child Survival and Safe Motherhood Programme (CSSM) was launched in 1992 as a part of the Family Welfare Programme, and this integrated all earlier health programmes. This programme primarily aims at reducing maternal morbidity and mortality, thereby ensuring child survival, through an integrated package of intervention. The CSSM programme was later merged with the on-going Reproductive and Child Health (RCH) programme in 1997, which aimed at improving the health status of young women and children by implementing client-centred, demand-driven quality health services. Under the RCH programme, safe motherhood initiative has got central attention and it has been realized that safe motherhood can be ascertained by providing a comprehensive package of maternal health services to all women during pregnancy, childbirth and the postpartum period.

Mother's healthcare during pregnancy, delivery and post-delivery form an important component in reducing low birth-weight babies and in reducing peri-natal, neo-natal and infant mortality. The Safe Motherhood Initiative proclaims that all pregnant women must receive basic professional antenatal care (Harrison, 1990). A pregnant woman can have an antenatal check-up by visiting a doctor or any other health professional in a medical facility and/or at home from a health worker, or both. The Reproductive and Child Health Programme recommends that as part of antenatal care, women should receive two doses of tetanus toxoid vaccine, adequate amounts of iron and folic acid tablets or syrup to prevent and treat anaemia. They should also have at least three antenatal check-ups that include blood pressure checks and other procedures to detect pregnancy complications (Ministry of Health and Family Welfare, 1997; 1998b).

The Population Policy statement of Madhya Pradesh (2000) mentions the set goal of increasing registration of pregnant women to 90 per cent by 2009; institutional delivery from 15 per cent in 1995 to 50 per cent; and 90 per cent deliveries to be assisted by trained birth attendants by 2011. The policy statement sets the goal of reducing maternal mortality from 498 per 100,000 live births in 1997 to 220 by 2011.The statement further reveals that the government will create pregnancy testing facilities at each sub-centre by 2003 and the necessary facilities in 50 per cent of block-level health institutions for emergency obstetric care, medical termination of pregnancy, and prevention and management of RTI/STI in all institutions by 2011.

**Objectives**

The aim of this proposed paper is to oversee the present scenario of safe motherhood programme in Madhya Pradesh.

The paper broadly covers the issues of antenatal, natal and postnatal care. The magnitudes of safe delivery and complications during pregnancy, delivery and post-delivery period have also been discussed. Further, this paper also critically looks at the possible changes in women's perception on the necessity of ANC services required during pregnancy. The paper proposes to compare Madhya Pradesh with other States and the country as a whole to see the current position of Madhya Pradesh in how far 'safe motherhood' has been achieved.

## Source of Data

The secondary data of National Family Health Survey (NFHS)-I (1992), and NFHS-II, (1998-99) and Reproductive and Child Health (RCH) Phase I and II (1998-99) have been used for the present study. NFHS-I and II data were collected from currently married women in the age group 15-49, while RCH data provides information from currently married women in the age group 15-44 representing both rural and urban segments of the population of the State.

## Review and Analysis

### *Antenatal Care (ANC)*

A pregnant woman can have an antenatal check-up by visiting a doctor another health professional in a medical facility, and/ or at home from a health-worker or both. The total ANC in Madhya Pradesh based on the reports of NFHS-II is 61.1 per cent, which is higher by 9 per cent point as compared to the NFHS-I (52.3 per cent) data. Both the survey results revealed that ANC coverage is notably higher in urban areas as compared to rural areas.

The net increase in the magnitude of ANC services is noticed with around 9 per cent point in almost six year duration. It has been expected that with the introduction of RCH programme, the outreach services will improve significantly through intensifying the home visits of health-workers. The data, however, revealed somewhat discouraging picture, showing a decline in ANC coverage at home from 16 per cent to 10 per cent (Fig. 7.1). If this difference is not significant, the data certainly attribute at least a "no change" in outreach ANC services largely covered by the health-workers (ANM). On the other hand, it has been noticed that a slightly higher more percentage of women have started approaching doctors and other health professionals for availing of ANC services.

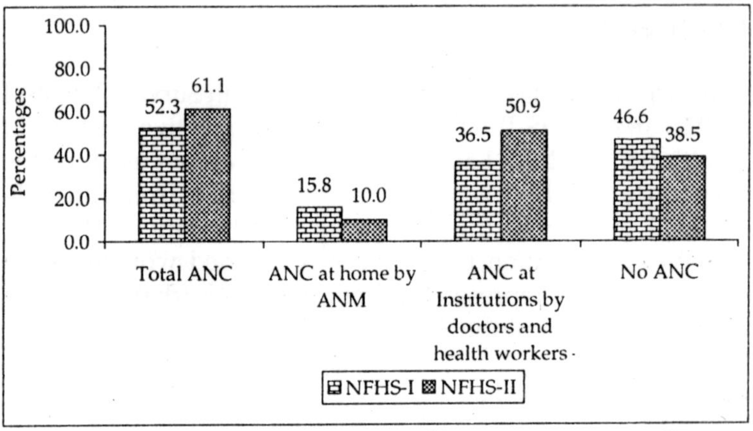


**Fig. 7.1:** Antenatal Care (ANC)

The outreach health services, including ANC services has been greatly affected by the poor frequency of home visits by the health-workers. According to NFHS-II report, overall, only 9 per cent of the women in Madhya Pradesh have been visited by government and /or private health-workers at home during past 12 months. RCH survey (1998-99) also gives almost comparable figure of ANM/LHV visit in rural areas.

According to the RCH survey, Madhya Paradesh has been ranked 12th among the 32 States and Union Territories in so far as health-workers' visit is concerned. This clearly reveals that the frequency of making home visits by MPHW is not adequate enough to meet the objective of extending primary health services at the outreach level. The meagre frequency of health-workers' visit could be due to several reasons like shortage of the required number of health-workers, inaccessibility and transportation problem. Lack of worker's motivation and negligence towards their job performance however, cannot be overlooked (Khan, 2003). This is where the programme has to evolve a viable and effective mechanism to improve the services at a peripheral level. The State has already initiated the steps for involving all stakeholders, particularly the Panchayati Raj Institutions, urban local bodies, the NGOs, Jan Swasth Rakshak, Mahila Swasth Sangh, Mahila Mandal and youth for community mobilization and participation in the family welfare programme.

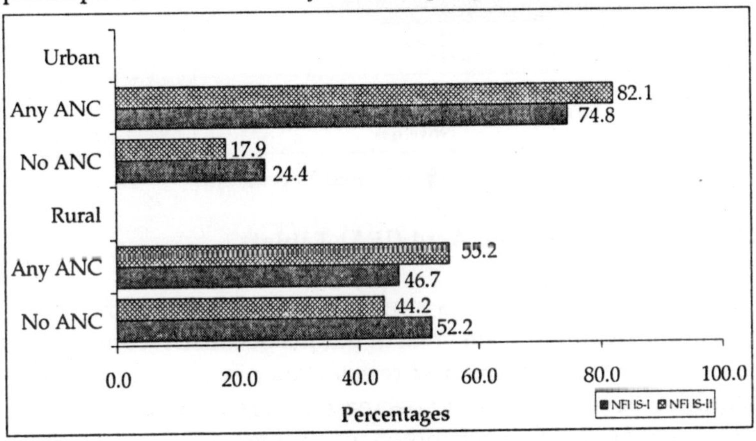


**Fig. 7.2:** Antenatal Care (ANC) by Residence

## Coverage of Tetanus Toxoid (TT) Vaccination

In India, an important cause of death in infancy is neo-natal tetanus, which is caused by newborn infants becoming infected by tetanus organisms, usually at the umbilical stump. Two doses of tetanus toxoid vaccine given one month apart during early pregnancy are nearly 100 per cent effective in preventing tetanus among both newborn infants and their mothers. Figure 7.3 shows that 55 per cent of the women received two or more doses of TT injection during their pregnancy period as per the NFHS-II report. Overall, TT coverage has gone up by 12 per cent point between the two surveys. Interestingly, the net increase is recorded is 13 per cent in rural areas as compared to the urban areas where the net increase is recorded at 7 per cent. This gives a positive sign of increasing outreach coverage for TT vaccination.

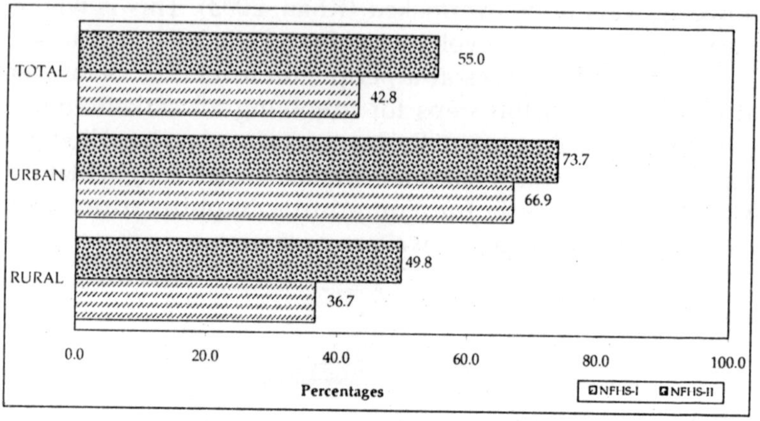


**Fig. 7.3:** Tetanus Toxoid Vaccination

## Coverage of Iron Folic Acid (IFA) Tablets

Iron deficiency anaemia is a major threat to safe motherhood and to the health and survival of infants because it contributes to low birth weight, lowered resistance to infection, impaired cognitive development and decreased work capacity. In order to prevent Iron deficiency, pregnant women are recommended to consume 100 iron and folic acid tablets during pregnancy. Figure 7.4 shows that in Madhya Pradesh, 49 per cent of the mothers received IFA supplements during pregnancy period indicating a net increase of about 5 per cent point. The increase is relatively higher in rural areas (5 per cent) as compared to the urban areas (2 per cent).

## Reasons for Not Seeking/Receiving Antenatal Check-up

Table 7.1 shows the per cent distribution of births in the three years preceding the survey whose mother did not receive any antenatal check-ups in the health facility or at home by the main reason for not receiving ANC check-ups. The table shows

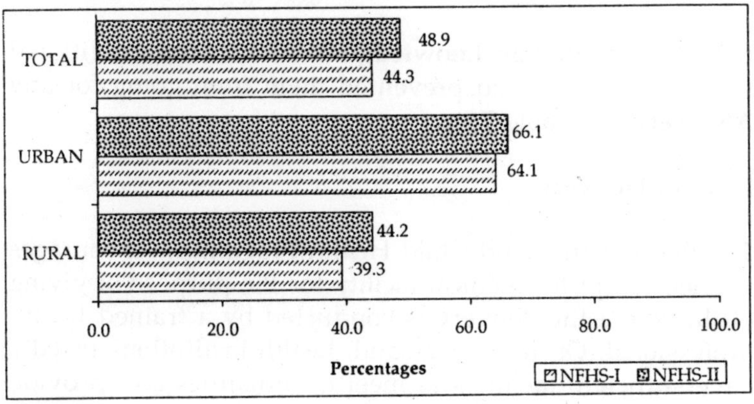


**Fig. 7.4:** Iron Folic Acid (IFA) Tablets

**Table 7.1:** Reasons for not Seeking/Receiving Antenatal Check-up

| *Reasons for not seeking/receiving antenatal care* | *NFHS-I* | *NFHS-II* |
|---|---|---|
| Lack of knowledge | 9.3 | 4.0 |
| Not necessary | 58.2 | 55.9 |
| Not customary | 5.1 | 2.8 |
| Financial cost | 7.3 | 16.4 |
| Inconvenient | 3.1 | 5.8 |
| Poor quality service | 0.5 | 0.8 |
| No time to go | 6.5 | 2.3 |
| Not permitted to go/family did not allow | 6.5 | 7.2 |
| No health-worker visited | — | 4.1 |
| Other | 1.0 | 0.7 |
| Number of Births | 1755 | 1093 |

more or less identical situation between NFHS-I and NFHS-II in terms of the reasons stated by them for not seeking or receiving antenatal care. Both for NFHS-I and NFHS-II, more than half of the mothers who did not have any antenatal check-ups felt that ANC in not necessary during pregnancy. This is so because pregnancy has always been considered a usual, rather than special phenomenon. For them, medical attention is not necessarily required during pregnancy. The reason for not receiving an antenatal check-up due to lack of knowledge has been reduced by 5 per cent point. These two opinions indicate that though knowledge has increased, traditional beliefs influenced and prevented them from going for any ANC services (Table 7.1).

**Place of Delivery**

The Reproductive and Child Health Programme encourages women to opt for medical facility for the purpose of giving birth, where the delivery is conducted by a trained health professional. On the other hand, health institutions usually have sufficient facilities to meet eventualities and provide emergency care. NFHS-II recorded 20 per cent institutional deliveries as against 16 per cent in NFHS-I survey, revealing the net increase of about four per cent point in institutional delivery (Fig. 7.5). The institutional delivery is much lower than the national average of 34 per cent for country as a whole. This has shown that the deliveries are by and large conducted at home.

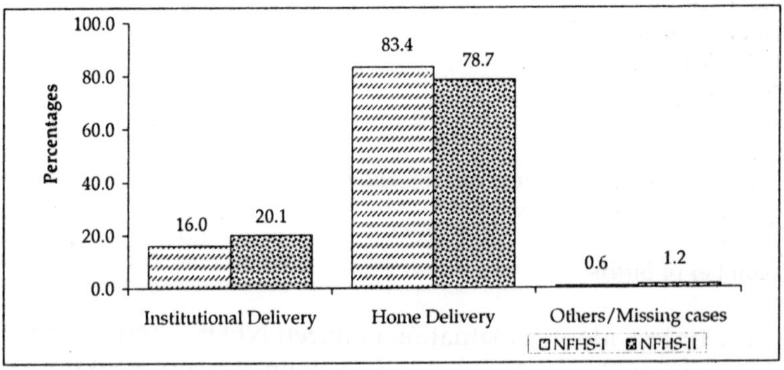


**Fig. 7.5:** Place of Delivery

**Assistance During Home Delivery**

There have been limitations and constraints in visiting health institutions for the purpose of delivery. Traditional practices of home delivery, poor transportation and access to health facilities, in addition to the financial implication are the major constraints not only in reaching health facilities for delivery but also at the time of seeking emergency obstetric care. In view of these constraints, the CSSM programme addressed the need of conducting home delivery in a safe environment. The Traditional Birth Attendant (TBA) known as *Dai* have been trained on the conduct of safe delivery by using a kit containing essential materials needed for conducting safe delivery. Both the NFHS surveys do not provide data for home delivery conducted by the trained TBA. The data, however, indicates that the percentage of TBA conducting home delivery has increased from 36 per cent to 59 per cent, while the percentage of delivery assisted by relatives has come down from 46 to 29 per cent (Fig. 7.6). The RCH data indicates that institutional delivery constitutes about 22 per cent and the rest are home deliveries in the State as a whole. Of the total home deliveries, only 11 per cent deliveries were conducted by trained TBA in the State, which is a little higher compared to the country as a whole (8 per cent). Though the RCH and NFHS surveys provide different figures in matters of home delivery, they have certainly pinpointed the limited role-played by trained TBA in conducting home deliveries, revealing a serious setback to the earlier CSSM programme.

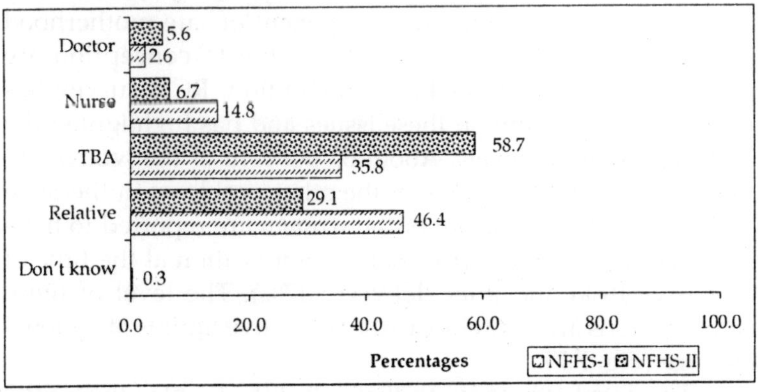


**Fig. 7.6:** Assistance during Home Delivery

## Safe Delivery

A delivery that has either been conducted at health institutions or at home and is fully assisted by the trained health personnel ensures safe delivery. The NFHS data suggests that there has been no change in the magnitude of safe delivery as both the NFHS surveys suggested 30 per cent safe delivery in the State, which is lower than the national average of about 42 per cent (Table 7.2). The RCH figure is very close to the NFHS indicating 28 per cent safe delivery for the State and 40 per cent for the country. The safe delivery recorded is highest in Kerala with 94 per cent and the lowest with 23 per cent in the State of Uttar Pradesh.

**Table 7.2:** Safe Delivery

| | *NFHS-I* | *NFHS-II* |
|---|---|---|
| India | - | 41.7 |
| Madhya Pradesh | 30.0 | 30.1 |
| Highest (Kerala) | 89.7 | 94.0 |
| Lowest (Uttar Pradesh) | 17.2 | 23.0 |

## Reproductive Morbidity and Treatment

Management of pregnancy, delivery and post-delivery complication is an important component of safe motherhood initiatives as most problems arising due to conception are treatable with timely medical intervention. RCH survey has collected information on these issues and has highlighted the treatment seeking levels. About 63 per cent of the women, in the State suffered from one or the other problems in the State while a little less than half of the women are reported to have said that they suffered from some complication at the time of delivery (46%) and after delivery (47%). The level of these complications are very close to the respective figures of national average (Fig. 7.7).

The data further reveals that only 39 per cent of those who reported to having pregnancy complications could seek treatment. Out of those who suffered from post-delivery complications, only 36 per cent of them could seek treatment. The survey clearly shows that the level of treatment seeking is noticeably lower within the State, compared to the national average.

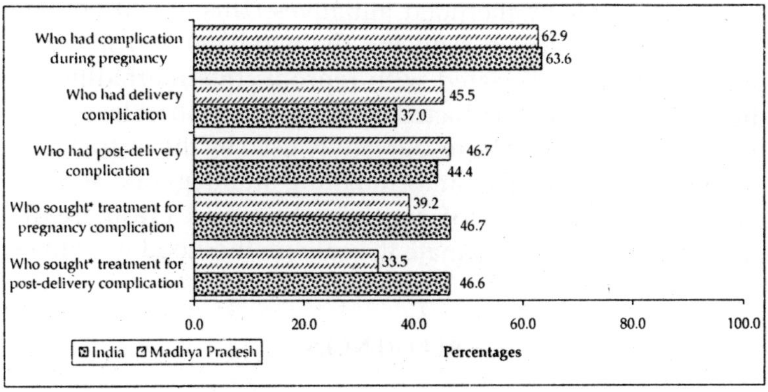


* Per cent refer to women who had complication.
*Source*: RCH Survey, Phase I and II (1998-99).

**Fig. 7.7:** Pregnancy, Delivery and Post-Delivery Complication and Treatment

## Discussion

The NFHS and RCH surveys have provided enormous data on the reproductive and child heath indicators not only at State level but also at district level. These surveys also provide the trend of progress over a period of time and are useful in district level planning and evaluation. As is evident from the data, safe motherhood indicators have not been redressed at the grassroots level in a manner at which the programme is likely to achieve the set goals. The existing networks of Government health facilities have been under-utilised and is unable to meet the full objective of safe motherhood initiatives. Under CSSM programme it was expected that the training of TBA would be the most effective strategy to ensure safe delivery in settings where home birth is the norm. There has been a serious setback in this strategy, as the role of trained TBA is limited and raises questions on the acceptability of trained TBA over untrained domiciliary birth attendants. Further investigation into dominant birthing belief and practices might answer some of these questions.

A viable strategy needs to be formulated in order to address the safe motherhood initiatives. This would perhaps be an effective step in reducing the neo-natal and maternal deaths that are associated with reproductive morbidity and the unsafe delivery conducted at home. The district level RCH survey results should be resourcefully used by the district level planners and managers in formulating an integrated strategy to achieve the goals of reproductive and child health programme that amalgamate the safe motherhood initiatives.

## REFERENCES

*Annual Report* (2000-2001), Department of Public Health and Family Welfare, Government of Madhya Pradesh.

Ministry of Health and Family Welfare (1998), *Manual in Community Needs Assessment Approach in Family Welfare Programme*, Department of Family Welfare, Ministry of Health and Family Welfare, Government of India.

International Institute of Population Sciences (IIPS), *National Family Health Survey-1* (1992), Madhya Pradesh (1992-93).

International Institute of Population Sciences (IIPS), and ORC Macro 2000 *National Family Health Survey-2*, Madhya Pradesh (1998-99).

Population Policy of Madhya Pradesh (2000), Department of Health and Family Welfare, Government of Madhya Pradesh. *Reproductive and Child Health Project—Rapid Household Survey Phase I and II*, India (1998-1999).

Khan, M.I. (2003), *"Quality of Health Communication and Family Welfare Services in Madhya Pradesh—An Overview and Future Challenges"* Paper presented in the seminar on Population of Madhya Pradesh, Organized by Population Resource Centre, Bhopal held on January 23-25, 2003.

# 8

# Challenges for Population Stabilization Programme

## A Critical Analysis of Acceptance of Male Contraceptive Methods in India

*Md. Irfan Khan* and *K.K. Verma*

### Introduction

India is the second largest populous country in the world after China. According to the census 2001 the total population of the country is 1027 millions and the projected figure for 2006 is 1094 millions. The projection indicates that by 2045 India's population will supercede China, if the annual exponential growth rate continues at the same pace.

India is the first country in the world, which had shown concern over the high growth rate of population. The State sponsored Family Planning Programme was launched as early as in 1951 during First Five Year Plan (1951-56). National health and population policies were formulated with short-term and long-term objectives to achieve a stable population. As a result Crude Birth Rate (CBR) had come down from 40.8 in 1951 to 25.8 in 2000, Infant Mortality Rate (IMR) from 146 per 1000 live birth to 68 in 2000, Crude Death Rate (CDR) from 25.1 to 8.5, Life Expectancy at Birth (LEB) from 37 to 62 and Total Fertility Rate (TFR) 6.1 in 1951 to 3.2 in 1999 (National Population Policy 2000). Contraceptive Prevalence Rate (CPR) due to modern method which was 10.4 in 1971 (ORG, 1971) has increased to 45.7 during 2002-2004 (DLHS-RCH 2006).

The National Population Policy laid stress on vigorously promoting the small family norm to achieve replacement level of TFR (2.1) by 2010 (National Population Policy 2000). The replacement fertility is expected to be achieved, if the CPR arrives at 60 per cent. Many Indian States have already achieved replacement fertility while there are States where CPR has gone above 60 per cent but the replacement fertility is not yet achieved due to the effect of population momentum.

Interestingly, the policies and the strategies which were adopted in India by and large laid stress on achieving Family Planning targets until 1996 through compulsion on the service providers. The approaches, however, created an unabridged gap between men and women in terms of the acceptability of contraception, be it a terminal or spacing method.

After the Cairo Conference in 1994 and Beijing Conference in 1995, the agenda of gender equality and male partnership were brought into sharp focus for population stabilization programme. It is in this context that a critical examination is essential for the population policies and programme inputs to control population growth rate. The critical analysis will help provide the way in which the changes in programmes and policies were brought about over the period of time and the goals that were achieved since India's Independence in 1947.

It is high time to review population stabilization programme gaps in the context of the gendered nature of Family Planning acceptance *A* combination of cultural factors and strategies together influence the rate of acceptance of Family Planning services. In the other words, one may say that *A* is the function of *C* and *S* denoted as

$$A \propto (C, S)$$

where "*A*" stands for degree of acceptance of contraceptive. "*C*" and "*S*" respectively are cultural factors influencing the acceptance and strategies adopted in the reference period. Any change in "*C*" or "*S*" will influence "*A*".

## Objective

The paper aims at examining the trend of male and female contraceptive acceptance in India. It critically overseas the dynamics between cultural factors and population stabilization programme.

### Sources of Data

The paper is based on the secondary data obtained from the all India Reproductive and Child Health, District Level Household Survey (2002-2004)[1], National Family Health Survey-I and II (1992-93 and 1998-1999)[2] and Family Planning Practices in India (1971, 1980 and 1988)[3]. In addition various documents and reports published by the Department of Family Welfare, Ministry of Health and Family Welfare, Government of India have also been used.

### Family Planning Programme and Induction of Contraceptives

In the first two Five Year Plans that is in 1951-56 and 1956-61 a clinical approach was followed to provide advise and services to the couples wishing to space and limit births. The number of Family Planning clinics rose from 59 in 1951 to 165 in 1956 and to 4134 by 1961 (Karkal,1998). Given a strong desire to space and limit family size, contraceptive services would be utilized if they were made available. It was towards the end of 1959 that vasectomy was added in the cafeteria approach of Family Planning Programme. Towards the end of the Second Five Year Plan a survey was undertaken to examine the effectiveness of clinics providing Family Planning services. The survey showed that the establishment of the service points were not adequate enough to motivate the couples. Contraceptives adopted were largely female methods. Male participation in the programme was negligible. This could also be seen as indicative of the patriarchal attitude of the programme planners at that time (Karkal, 1988).

The approach to Family Planning in Third Five Year Plan (1961-66) shifted to extension of education, wherein the clinical staff were to work in the community. Information, Education and Communication (IEC) approach was adopted in the programme. IUD and sterilization—the two clinical methods were made available. During this period financial incentives were introduced to Family Planning acceptors. Out of pocket expenses, conveyance and loss of wages were provided to the acceptors. In addition a little financial incentives were given to the health staff. The programme gained momentum during 1966-67 by making it target oriented programme. Srinivasan (1995) called it as Low Intensity HITTS model, i.e. Health Department operated, Incentive-based, Target-oriented, Time bound and Sterilization focused programme. This was the beginning of HITTS approach which lasted until 1977 with varying degree of emphasis on each of its components of involvement of health functionaries, change of incentives, target and the time frame of achievement of the targets. Vasectomy was preferred over other available Family Planning methods as a population stabilization device (Srinivasan, 2006: 7-8). Small and large Vasectomy camps were organized during the period from 1969 to 1977. Both cash and kind incentives were given to the accepters, the motivators and the health staff.

A vaginal tubectomy technique was introduced in 1970. Till 1970, female sterilization could be performed only during the post-partum period in the clinic. Development of the technique facilitated organizing tubectomy at camps in rural and urban areas.

In April 1976, the First National Population Policy was passed by the Indian Parliament. Government of India at that time considered it as frontal attack on the problem of population. It turned out to be a coercive approach, ignoring the rights of people. The incentive payments to acceptors were substantially increased. Innovative political and fiscal incentives were offered by the Government of India to the State to implement the Family Planning Programme. Vasectomies and tubectomies were performed during 1976-77 on war footing and 8.26 million sterilizations were done during this period. However, the new Government, which came to power after emergency period changed the name of Family Planning to 'family welfare' programme in 1977 and adopted a New Population Policy. In the New Policy emphasis was given on educational programme, freedom of choice and contraceptive methods.

Again, change in Central Government in 1980, brought about a change in the population policy. The emphasis on sterilization continued in post-1980s on a voluntary basis. Laparoscopic technique was introduced in early 1980s and tubal ligation became more convenient while acceptance of vasectomy continue to remain low since 1977.

Men almost refused to come forward for vasectomy in spite of growing desire for small family size. As a result of this and due to the lack of easy availability of spacing methods, sterilization of women began to rise. Partial reason for the same had roots in the Indian patriarchal social structure.

The period, post-1980s witnessed the revival of health based, time-bound, target-oriented Family Planning Programme with reduced emphasis on sterilization and increased emphasis on spacing methods and child survival. Attempt was made to link fertility goal to mortality level through adoption of achievable level of net reproduction rate. In subsequent five year plan periods, short and long-term goals were set.

Post-1990s witnessed notable events in the country, as enactment of Panchayati Raj in 1992, submission of Swaminathan Committee report on population in 1994 and organization of International Conferences on Population Policies and Programmes at Cario. Government has abolished the acceptor based Family Planning target in 1996. Since 1997, officially the Reproductive and Child Health (RCH) approach has been adopted as a national policy.

Taking a note of the aforesaid events and situation, National Population Policy, 2000 and National Health Policy, 2002 have been adopted and enforced. In 2005, National Rural Health Mission (NRHM) has been launched to improve quality of life in the country to bring rural health programme in mission mode. However, till today the responsibility of Family Planning lies with the Government. It is yet to get transferred to individual families (Zodgekar, 1996: 24).

### Trend in Contraceptive Acceptors

The Government of India provides data on Couples Effectively Protected (CEP) and percentage of Couple Currently Protected

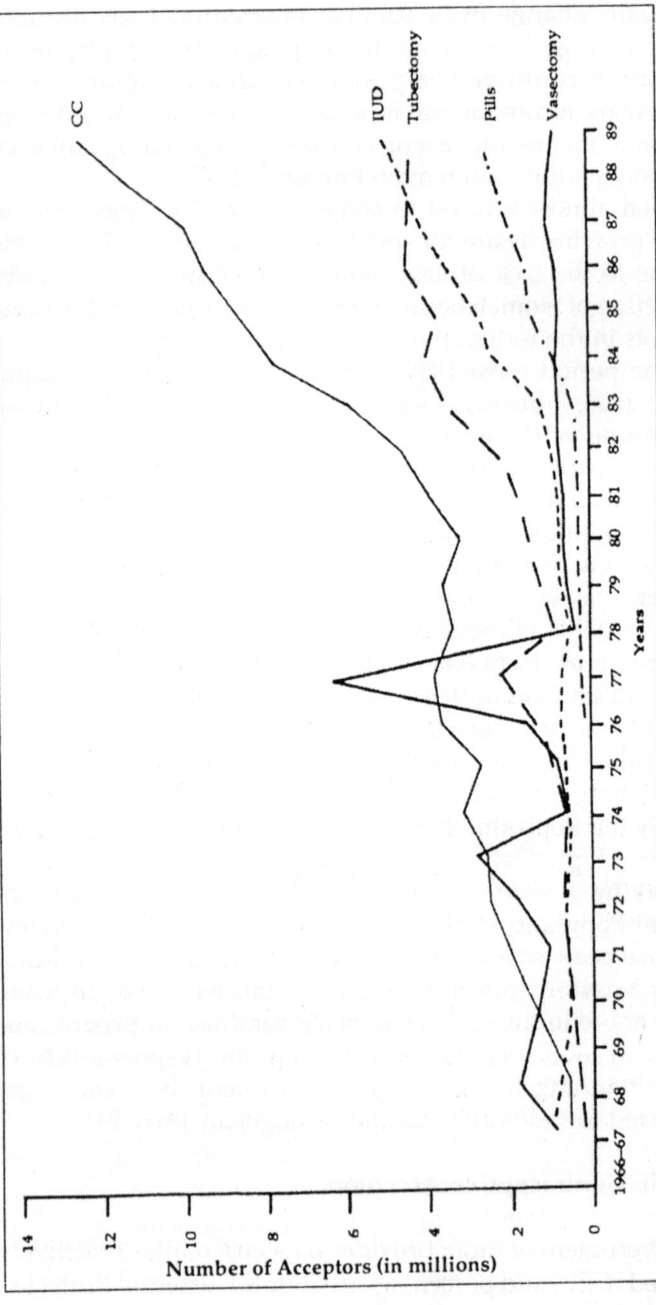


*Source*: Year Book 1990-91, Family Welfare Programme in India, MOH&FW, Department of Family Welfare (1992).

**Fig. 8.1:** Year-wise Family Planning Performance: India (1966-90)

(CCP) in a given year. CCP in a given year therefore is calculated by adding current year acceptors and previous year acceptors after deducting dropouts due to various reasons. The modern spacing methods are converted to equivalent sterilization for that particular year. For example, the number of sterilizations is equivalent to 1/3 the number of IUD insertion, 1/18 the number of equivalent condom users and 1/9 the number of equivalent oral pill users for CEP calculation. It is to be noted that the number of acceptors is estimated on the basis of number of units of contraceptives distributed to the population at various service delivery points. The number of condom distributed is divided by 72, pills cycles by 13, foam tablets by 72 and jelly/cream by 3 to get average number of non-clinical contraceptive users in a year. Figures 8.1 and 8.2 provide official statistics on yearly contraceptive users during 1966-90 and 1990-2001 respectively.

Figure 8.1 indicates vasectomy as a dominant contraceptive method until 1977. The same dropped drastically in 1978. It is evident that the Post-Emergency phase, which is known as recovery phase changed the statistics of the acceptors in which vasectomy remained as low as 0.254 million against 3.87 million tubectomy/laparoscopy during 1990-91.

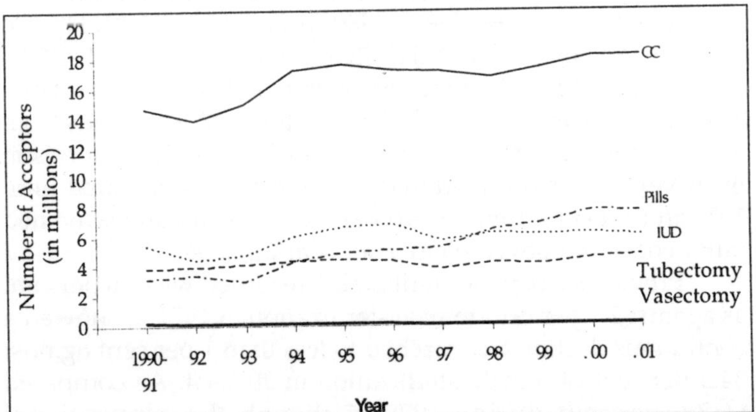


*Source*: Year Book 2001, Family Welfare Programme in India, MOH&FW, Department of Family Welfare (2003).

**Fig. 8.2:** Year-wise Family Planning Performance: India (1991-2001)

The acceptors of modern spacing methods like IUD, Pills and CC increased manifold after 1990. The official statistics as shown in Fig. 8.2 indicates that vasectomy acceptors started declining further after 1996. The absolute number of vasectomy performed during 2000-2001 was in decimal figures of million (0.109 million) against 4.62 million laproscopy/tubectomy. At the same time acceptance of modern spacing methods in effect continued to go up. However, the rise of CC users may be interpreted with caution as the figure is estimated on the quantum of distribution of condom through various health services outlets and depots. The distribution does not guarantee the actual usage of CC for the purpose of Family Planning *per se*. The absolute rise in CC acceptors may be partly attributed to the campaign for HIV/AIDS prevention through safe sex in last one decade.

### Contraceptive Prevalence Rate (CPR)

The official statistics as shown in Fig. 8.1 and Fig. 8.2 provide absolute number of acceptors after converting the total number of contraceptive distributed by fixed number.

The First All India Family Planning Survey, conducted by ORG in 1970-71 provided the State and National level CPR. The other surveys (*See* ORG, 1980-81 and 1988-89, NFHS-I in 1992-93, NFHS-II and DLHS-RCH in 1998-99, DLHS-RCH, 2002-04) provided the time series data on CPR over the time. The CPR increased due to modern contraceptive methods from 9.7 per cent in 1971 to 54.7 per cent in 2002-04. A comparison of survey results revealed that male methods dominated until 1971 and a reverse trend was observed afterward and remained fairly constant between 5 to 6 per cent till 2004.

Prevalence of male sterilization recorded was 3.6 per cent as against 2.7 per cent female sterilization in 1971. It showed a continuous decline and reached to less than 1 per cent against 34.3 per cent of female sterilization in 2002-04. As compared to 2.6 per cent during 1970-71 though the conventional contraceptive (CC) or condom usage increased until 1988-89 to the tune of 5 per cent and started declining in early 90s. (1992-93). It regained momentum to 3.1 per cent in 1998-99 and 4.8 per cent in 2002-04 (Table 8.1).

**Table 8.1:** Trends of Modern Contraceptive Prevalence Rate

| *FP Methods* | *1970-71* | *1980-81* | *1988-89* | *1992-93* | *1998-99* | *2002-04* |
|---|---|---|---|---|---|---|
| **Any Method** | 13.6 | 35.0 | 44.9 | 40.6 | 48.2 | 53.0 |
| **Any Modern Method** | 9.7 | 28.0 | 39.9 | 36.3 | 42.8 | 45.7 |
| **Terminal Method** | 6.3 | 22.0 | 31.3 | 30.7 | 36.1 | 35.2 |
| Vasectomy | 3.6 | NA | NA | 3.4 | 1.9 | 0.9 |
| Tubectomy | 2.7 | NA | NA | 27.3 | 34.2 | 34.3 |
| **Spacing Method** | 3.6 | 6.0 | 8.6 | 5.5 | 6.8 | 10.2 |
| IUD | 0.7 | 0.0 | 1.9 | 1.9 | 1.6 | 1.9 |
| Pills | 0.3 | 1.0 | 1.4 | 1.2 | 2.1 | 3.5 |
| Condom | 2.6 | 5.0 | 5.3 | 2.4 | 3.1 | 4.8 |

NA = Not Available.

The condom, oral pills and IUD used increased in past one decade due to the impact of paradigm shift under RCH programme. The RCH programme focuses on client-centred, demand-driven and target-free integrated quality services at the grassroots level. The female sterilization remains constant after 1998 to the tune of 35 per cent or almost three-fourth share of the total Family Planning.

## Gender Inequality in Contraceptive Acceptability

Table 8.2 summarizes gender inequality in the acceptability of modern contraceptive methods. The gender specific acceptability of contraceptives has been taken into consideration in terms of male contraceptive use and female contraceptive use. The male contraceptive use combined conventional vasectomy/No scalpel vasectomy and condom while female contraceptive use includes tubectomy/laproscopy, IUD and Pills. Evidently, India's Family Planning Programme took a U-turn in favour of female methods in 1977. Since then, the male partnership in contraceptive acceptance has come down to 5.7 per cent (which includes 0.9 per cent vasectomy and 4.8 per cent condom) against 39.7 use of female contraceptives (Table 8.2).

Figure 8.3, summarizes State-wise gender specific use of contraceptive methods. Overall trend in terms of differential rate of acceptance of male and female contraceptive is same as that for the nation. This trend is not different among the

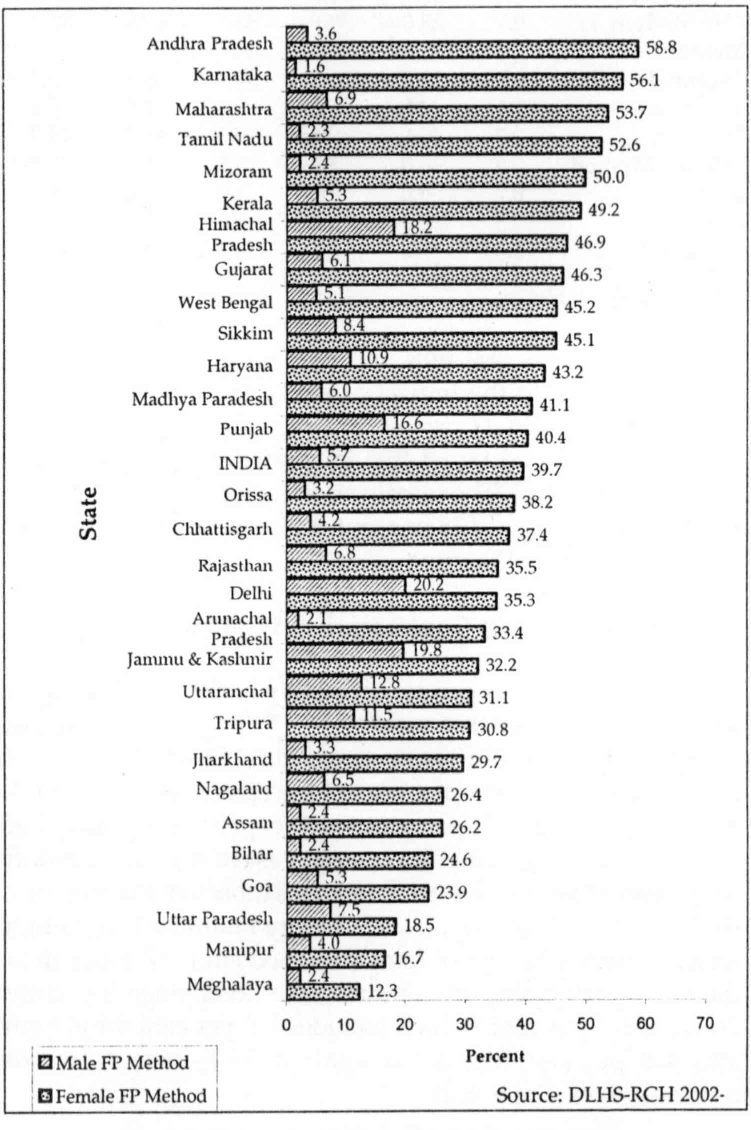


**Fig. 8.3:** State-wise CPR by Gender Specific Usage

educationally advanced State like Kerala and Mizoram, industrially advanced States like Gujarat and Maharastra and agriculturally advanced States like Punjab and Haryana. A close look on the State variation by gender specific contraceptive acceptance indicates that Delhi and Punjab have shown a relatively higher acceptance of male contraceptive methods precisely due to higher use of condom and not the vasectomy.

**Table 8.2:** Trends of Modern Contraceptive Prevalence Rate by Gender Specific Usage

| *Gender Specific Usage* | *1970-71* | *1992-93* | *1998-99* | *2002-04* |
|---|---|---|---|---|
| Female | 3.7 | 30.4 | 37.9 | 39.7 |
| Male | 6.2 | 5.8 | 5.0 | 5.7 |
| **Total** | **9.7** | **36.3** | **42.8** | **45.7** |

### Introduction of No Scalpel Vasectomy (NSV)

No Scalpel Vasectomy (NSV) technology was introduced in India's Population Stabilization Programme during the last quarter of 1997-98. Facility to perform No Scalpel Vasectomy (NSV) has been made available at selected district hospitals and health clinics. The RCH survey conducted during 2002-04 indicated that one-third of the male respondent (33.6%) had heard of NSV (Table 8.3). About 22.8 per cent respondents considered NSV simpler to conventional vasectomy. 16.9 per cent of them opined that it would create no complication. A sizeable percentage (14.2 per cent) believed that NSV does not affect a man's sexual performance—a myth carried through generations. In spite of the fact that the method has the potential to increase the male acceptance of Family Planning, the service is yet to be universalized.

**Table 8.3:** Awareness of No Scalpel Vasectomy (NSV)

| *Awareness of NSV* | *Rural* | *Urban* | *Total* |
|---|---|---|---|
| Heard of NSV | 29.4 | 42.9 | 33.6 |
| NSV is simpler to conventional vasectomy | 19.8 | 29.5 | 22.8 |
| NSV has no complication | 14.6 | 22.1 | 16.9 |
| NSV does not affect man's sexual performance | 12.0 | 19.2 | 14.2 |
| Number of Men | 228077 | 102742 | 330819 |

*Source*: DLHS-RCH, 2002-04.

## Sources of Family Planning Services

Family welfare services are provided to the community through a network of health Sub-Centres (SC), Primary Health Centres (PHC), Community Health Centres (CHC) in rural areas and district hospitals and dispensaries including Urban Family Welfare Centres (UFWC) and Urban Health Post (UHP) in urban areas. This network was setup under Basic Minimum Services (BMS) programme. As on March 31, 2001, 137311 Sub-Centres, 22842 PHCs and 3042 CHCs were functioning in the country (Year Book, 2001).

**Table 8.4:** Sources of Family Planning Services

| *FP Methods* | *Government* | | *Private* | | *Others (Shop)* | |
|---|---|---|---|---|---|---|
| | *1992-93* | *1998-99* | *1992-93* | *1998-99* | *1992-93* | *1998-99* |
| OCP | 31.0 | 20.6 | 41.5 | 40.6 | 27.4 | 35.5 |
| IUD | 62.9 | 54.1 | 35.8 | 43.1 | 1.6 | 2.5 |
| Condom | 15.2 | 13.9 | 20.3 | 39.3 | 64.5 | 37.9 |
| Female Sterilization | 86.1 | 85.3 | 13.3 | 13.1 | 0.6 | 1.2 |
| Male Sterilization | 93.4 | 88.6 | 4.3 | 8.9 | 2.3 | 2.0 |
| All Modern Methods | 79.0 | 76.0 | 15.0 | 17.3 | 6.0 | 5.6 |

*Source*: NFHS-I and NFHS-II.

The surveys revealed that Family Planning sterilization services are largely availed from Government health facilities both in rural and urban areas. However, the services for non-clinical methods like OCP and condom are availed from private health facilities including commercial outlets like medical and grocery shops. A close observation of Table 8.4 indicates that the people are shifting from Government to private health facilities for availing services for all the modern methods of Family Planning. Commercial outlets have been the second largest source of the OCP supply as it has increased from 27.4 per cent point in 1992-93 to 35.5 per cent in 1998-99. The condom supply has declined by almost 27 per cent point during the same period and users have shifted to private sources. ORG survey, way back in 1988-89 had indicated the same situation for the supply of oral pills and condom (58.6 per cent oral pills and 65.4 per cent condom users bought contraceptives from shops).

**Summing Up**

The dynamics of population stabilization, Family Planning policies and strategies indicates a 'gender bias' both interms of adoption of policies and strategies and social acceptability. The outcome clearly indicates that the Family Planning Programme has over burdened the women with contraceptive weights.

The patriarchal social structure in India encourages to have atleast one male child in a family. Consequently female contraceptives, were perhaps given more space in the Family Planning package even during early cafeteria approach. This was partly due to the assumption that the Indian society would favour female method over other that impair woman's reproductive decision reducing their rights to protect their own life and those of their probable offspring. The other reason of stressing female contraceptive was due to gender bias of the planners.

The coercive strategy of the Government during emergency period (1975-76) to control population at any cost led to large scale vasectomies and tubectomies in the country. To nullify the adverse effects in 1977 the programme of population stabilization was made wholly voluntary. Acceptability of male contraceptive in post-1977 period has gone down sharply whereas there is a constant increase in number of tubectomies. In other words female methods have been endorsed by 39.7 per cent against male methods by 5.7 per cent only.

The differential acceptance of contraceptive (more female than male) indicates an acceptance of male dominance in society. Analysis indicates that the contraceptive prevalence rate has already reached 45.7 per cent in which female participation is 87.0 per cent. Acceptance of male contraceptive is minimal at 13.0 per cent. The women were compelled to opt for contraception to meet the couple's desire for small family size against UN convention of elimination of all forms of discrimination against women rectified by Indian Government.

Technology of No-Scalpel Vasectomy (NSV) has been included recently in the family planning package, which needs to be propagated with the help of intensive IEC campaign and enhance services at PHC level. The stress for male participation in the Family Planning needs to be vigorously made through public-private partnership efforts. The hindering social and cultural factors and patriarchal attitude of people need to be carefully tackled by creating a national consensus and removing gender inequality in the present family welfare programme to achieve india's population stabilization goals.

### *Acknowledgments*

The authors gratefully acknowledge Dr. Binod C. Agrawal, Director and Professor Chandragupth Sanon of TALEEM for their encouragement and valuable suggestions in preparing this paper. The authors are also thankful to Ms. Ruchi Tewari for her editorial support and Mr. Vijay Uttekar fcr typing and graphic presentation of this paper.

## NOTES

1. Reproductive and Child Health Survey (2002-2004): The aim of the DLHS-RCH survey in India was to collect the district level information on reproductive and child healthcare indicators in order to strengthen and decentralized planning and implementation of the programme. The survey was conducted in two phases during 2002-2004 covering all the districts of the country. The survey covered 620107 households, 507622 currently married women age 15-44 and 330820 husbands of the eligible women spread across 593 districts of all 35 States and Union Territories. A total of twelve research organizations were involved in conducting the survey the nodal agency was IIPS, Mumbai, India.
2. National Family Health Survey-I (NFHS-I, 1992-93) and (NFHS-II, 1998-99): NFHS-I covered 89777 ever married women from among 88562 households in the age group 13-49 from 1405 urban units and 2117 rural units spread across 25 States. Similarly, NFHS-II covered 91196 households and 89199 ever married women age 15-49 spread

across 25 States. A total of 1021 urban and 2144 rural Primary Sample Units (PSUs) were selected for the survey.

3. Family Planning Practices in India (1971, 1980 and 1988): The first all India Survey (1971) was covered 25330 currently married individuals (12716 husband and 12614 wife) spread across 254 urban and 704 rural settlements. In the third round a total of 44918 couples spread across 205 towns and 1271 villages were covered. These three rounds of survey were carried by ORG, Baroda.

## REFERENCES


International Institute for Population Sciences, Mumbai, March, 2006, Reproductive and Child Health District Level Household Survey (DLHS-RCH, 2002-04), India Summary Report.

Karkal, Malini (1988), Family Planning and the Reproductive Rights of Women in Lakshmi Lingam (ed.) *Understanding Women's Health Issues*, SNDT, Mumbai.

*National Population Policy-2000*, Ministry of Health and Family Welfare, Government of India, New Delhi.

*National Family Health Survey (1992-93), India*, International Institute for Population Sciences, Mumbai, 1995.

*National Family Health Survey (1998-99)*, India, International Institute for Population Sciences, Mumbai, 2000

ORG (1971), Family Planning Practices in India: First All India Survey Report. Baroda (1983), Family Planning Practices in India: Second All India Survey Report, Baroda.

ORG (1990), Family Planning Practices in India: Third All India Survey Report, Baroda

Reproductive and Child Health District Level Household Survey (DLHS-RCH, 2002-04), International Institute for Population Sciences, Mumbai, August, 2006

Srinivasan, K. (1995), *Regulating Reproduction in India's Population—Efforts, Results and Recommendations*, Sage Publicaiton New Delhi (2006), Population Policies and Family Planning Programme in India—Review and Recommendations, *Newslatter*, No. 1 and 2, Volume 47, IIPS, Mumbai.

Year Book (2001), Family Welfare Programme in India, Department of Family Welfare, Ministry of Health and Family Welfare, Government of India, New Delhi, April 2003.

Zodgekar, Arvind (1996), Family Welfare Programme and Population Stabilization Strategies in India, *Asia-Pacific Population Journal*, Vol. XI (1).

# 9

# Status of Women and Fertility

*Mitali Chakrabarty*

## Introduction

Population explosion is a serious concern for India. One of the major constraints hampering India's overall development process is the increase in population. The effect of fertility has a great influence in the growth of population in a country. The fertility of women has always been a matter of vital concern not only to women themselves but also to the communities to which they belong (Thompson, 1953). The policy-makers are taking various measures for reducing fertility. India is a vast country with diverse communities, religious and cultural backgrounds. Anthropologists are interested in focusing on the cultural variation of different communities so as to help policy-makers to plan and adopt appropriate strategies in reducing fertility, keeping in mind the cultural values of that community.

Fertility studies on tribal population of India are not many and there is still less data on matriarchal population, where women enjoy higher status. The Jaintias of the Jaintia Hills district of the State of Meghalaya in India is the best example existing today of a society, which is matriarchal. They trace their descent from a female ancestress. They reckon their descent from the mother that is along the female lines. The youngest daughter inherits property from the mother. The earnings of the male members go to their mothers' family. The matrilocal residence, matrilineal descent and inheritance of property through the female line, which add to the status of women, also exists among the Khasis and the Garos of the same State. The Jaintias are unique, because they have traditionally an altogether different system of marriage, the **'Night Visit Marriage System'** (NVS), in which the husband comes to his wife's house after dusk and leaves for his mother's house before dawn and maintains this practice for as long as the marriage bond remains. In such a practice, the husband need not look after his children. As a matter of fact, the husband's role in his wife's family is only biological. But with the advent of Christianity, urbanization and modernization, this system of marriage is loosing its ground. Considering these points of view, it is proposed to undertake the study on fertility among the Jaintia tribal population of two selected rural areas and the only urban area of the Jaintia Hills districts in Meghalaya.

Jaintia Hills district is one of the seven districts of Meghalaya. It is situated between 25°8′ and 26°8′ North Latitude and between 92° and 92°51′ East Longitude. The altitude of the district varies from 1220 metres to 1830 metres above the sea level.

Traditionally, the Jaintias are animists. Their traditional religion is known as the Niamtre. Quite a good number of the Jaintias are found to have professed Christianity. Some of the Jaintias were converted to Hinduism in the distant past under the patronage of the Jaintia King. They are found only in one village, namely Nartiang.

The marriage bond between husband and wife among the Jaintias is loose. If a girl stays with a man and conceives, they are socially recognized as wife and husband so long they continue that tie. This relationship may be broken by two means: (a) by mutual consent of the two married partners without going through any formal procedure, and (b) they may divorce formally in the presence of a priest. After that one may remarry if he or she desires to do so.

## Aim of the Study

The main aim of the present study is to investigate the effect of higher status of women on fertility. The present study also aims to study the following aspects:

1. To observe rural-urban difference in fertility,
2. To look into the variations on fertility between different religious groups,
3. To see the effect of education on fertility, as it is believed that in the matrilineal society wives' educational status plays an important role in influencing fertility, and
4. To assess the impact of visit marriage system and multiple marriages on fertility.

**Area and Sample of the Study**

This study is based on the data collected from two rural areas, namely Nartiang and Mihmyntdu villages and from the only urban centre, Jowai during 1992-93.

The aforesaid two rural areas and the urban area were selected with a specific purpose to study the socio-cultural variation of the Jaintias in both rural and urban areas and amongst three religious groups.

The village Nartiang is a historically important place in the district as it is the only village in the district inhabited by the Hindu Jaintias. Along with the Hindu Jaintias there are Christian Jaintias also. A few Niamtre Jaintias, who have migrated from the neighbouring villages, are also found to reside in the village.

The village Mihmyntdu is inhabited mostly by the Niamtre Jaintias. Some Christian Jaintia families are also found in the village.

A total of 847 numbers of households (431 from the urban area and 416 from the rural areas) were surveyed. Altogether 1091 (554 from the rural areas and 537 from the urban area) numbers of ever married Jaintia women were interviewed following the questionnaire method. A structured schedule method was used to collect information on fertility. In addition, the case study method was followed in order to support some of the information with evidence.

## Findings and Discussion

Table 9.1 shows average number of live births to women based on residence and religion.

**Table 9.1:** Average Live Births to Women Based on Residence and Religion

| *Residence* | *Religion* | *No. of Women* | *No. of Live Births* | *Average No. of Live Births* |
|---|---|---|---|---|
| Rural | Hindu | 186 | 896 | 4.82 |
| | Niamtre | 185 | 914 | 4.94 |
| | Christian | 160 | 785 | 4.91 |
| | **Rural Total** | **531** | **2595** | **4.89** |
| Urban | Niamtre | 227 | 1095 | 4.82 |
| | Christian | 292 | 1160 | 3.97 |
| | **Urban Total** | **519** | **2255** | **4.34** |
| | **Grand Total** | **1050** | **4850** | **4.62** |

Many studies have been conducted on fertility based on rural-urban residence. The studies of Agarwala (1972), Sample Registration System (1976-78), Bhende *et al.* (1988) showed that fertility in the urban area is lower than that in the rural areas. The present study also shows that fertility is lower in the urban area (4.34) than that in the rural areas (4.89). The obvious reason is that the various facilities like education, medical and family planning devices are available in the urban area.

Some of the studies conducted in India (Bhende *et al.* 1988; Gulati, 1988) stated that religion is considered an important factor affecting fertility. Other studies conducted (Bhende *et al.* 1988; Krishnan, 1986) showed lower fertility rate among Christians compared to that of the Hindus and Muslims in India. The present study in the urban area reflects lower fertility to the Christian women (3.97) than to women belonging to the Niamtre religion (4.82). In rural areas, though fertility of the Christian women (4.91) is lower than that of the Niamtre (non-Christian) women (4.94), however, fertility of the Hindu women (4.82) is the lowest of all. Higher educational level might be the cause of reducing fertility among Christians.

The effect of education on fertility has been reported in many studies. According to most of the studies conducted in India, the effect of education in reducing fertility has been observed among the women having higher education (UN, 1961; Driver, 1963; Hussain, 1970 a, 1970 b; Nayar, 1986; Bharati *et al.* 1990). The present study also supports the earlier findings that fertility decreases with increasing educational level of women, irrespective of rural-urban difference (Table 9.2). Cadwell and McDonald (1981) are of the opinion that the level of education of mothers is a tool, which helps them in breaking some of the traditional norms and making them relatively more independent in taking decisions within the family situation. Bhende, *et al.* (1988) stated that the difference in the fertility performance arising out of the educational status of women may be mainly due to two factors; the differential age at marriage and the higher level of education providing higher level of information about keeping fertility under control and motivating the women to keep the family size small.

**Table 9.2:** Average Live Births Based on Educational Status of Women

| *Educational Status of Women* | *Average Number of Live Births* | | |
|---|---|---|---|
| | *Rural* | *Urban* | *Total* |
| Illiterate | 5.33 | 5.37 | 5.34 |
| Upto Class VI | 3.69 | 4.81 | 4.20 |
| Class VII to X | 3.65 | 4.00 | 3.93 |
| Matriculate and above | 3.33 | 3.67 | 3.65 |
| Graduate and above | 0.0 | 3.46 | 3.46 |

The status of women is known to have important implications for fertility performance. Studies of Agarwala (1972), Hari (1991), Mahadevan, *et al.* (1987) have shown that fertility declines with the raising in the status of women. Weller (1969) found that wives manifest lower fertility behaviour in wife-dominant and egalitarian families rather than in husband-dominant families. According to Mahadevan *et al.* (1987), "an increase in the level of emancipation of women significantly depresses fertility behaviour, irrespective of all other factors.

Since more Kerala women have a high level of emancipation and low fertility, the emancipation of women *per se* has significantly contributed to the decline of fertility in the Kerala village". However, the present study among the Jaintias, do not corroborate with the findings of Weller (1969) and Mahadevan *et al.* (1987). As referred to earlier, the Jaintia society is matriarchal and the women enjoy very high status in the society, more particularly in decision-making. The wife takes the final decision regarding the determination of size of the family. The husbands have no role to play in decision-making. Traditionally husbands do not stay with their wives and also do not look after their children. After dusk the husbands come to their wives' house, stay together for the night and leave before dawn. So, the maintenance of the family is the responsibility of the wives. A society having so high status for the women also has much higher fertility (4.62) than that of Kerala women (2.9) and Andhra women (3.3), as studied by Mahadevan *et al.* (1987) and that of women in Nellore town of Andhra Pradesh (2.03) (Hari, 1991). It is apparent from the above discussion that higher status of women alone cannot reduce the fertility of a population.

Table 9.3 reveals higher fertility of women following NVS (4.94 ± 0.06) than that to the women not following NVS (4.34 ± 0.05). Similar results have been observed in the rural as well as in the urban area and among all the religious groups. It is difficult to explain the causes of such variation in fertility. It has been discussed earlier that in 'visit marriage system', husband comes to his wife's house only at night and returns to his mother's house in the morning. His role in his wife's house is only biological. The husband has no responsibility of maintaining his family nor to look after his children. Moreover, husbands remain detached from their wives for whole day. In such a situation, perhaps the biological urge becomes dominant over emotional attachment, which may lead to higher fertility among them.

**Table 9.3:** Fertility of Women Based on Marriage System

| *Marriage System* | *Number of Women* | *Number of Live Births* | *Mean Live Births ± SE* |
|---|---|---|---|
| Women following NVS | 490 | 2422 | 4.94 ± 0.06 |
| Women not following NVS | 560 | 2428 | 4.34 ± 0.05 |

NVS — Night Visit Marriage System.

Table 9.4 shows that fertility of women married once (4.50 ± 0.05) is lower than that of the women married more than once (5.11 ± 0.07). Cases of divorce are not rare among the Jaintias. After divorce, women remarry. There are numbers of women who are found to marry more than three to four times. Remarriage reduces the duration of married life. Despite that fact, among them fertility is found to be higher. After every remarriage they may desire to have some more children from the new husband. New married life may also accelerate the biological urge to some extent. This may lead to higher fertility among them.

**Table 9.4:** Fertility of Women Based on Number of Marriage/s

| *Marriage System* | *Number of Women* | *Number of Live Births* | *Mean Live Births ± SE* |
|---|---|---|---|
| Women married once | 842 | 3788 | 4.50 ± 0.05 |
| Women married more than once | 208 | 1062 | 5.11 ± 0.07 |

From the above discussion it is observed that the Jaintia women, despite their enjoying higher social status show higher fertility. No single factor can be held responsible for higher fertility. However, education of women plays an important role in reducing fertility.

Unlike in patriarchal societies, the Jaintias desire more daughters, since they belong to a matriarchal society. It is observed from Tables 9.5a and 9.5b that the Jaintia women of both rural and urban areas, irrespective of their religious background, majority of the women reported to continue to bear two or more daughters, if the first child is a son. It may be because the Jaintias consider two or more daughters as a good sign and a good fortune for the family and also due to the prevailing system that the youngest daughter has to continue the family lineage and look after her parents in their old age. Several reasons were reported by the women for their preference of more daughters, among which, common reasons are:

(i) To continue the lineage,
(ii) To increase family/clan members and to increase the population size of the Jaintia tribes,
(iii) More daughters are regarded as a good sign and good fortune,

**Table 9.5a:** Distribution of Couples According to Values Regarding Additional Child if the First Child is a Son

| *Values regarding additional child if the first child is a son* | *Percentage Distribution of Couples* | | |
|---|---|---|---|
| | *Rural* | *Urban* | *Total* |
| Continue until birth of one daughter | 0.18 | 5.40 | 2.75 |
| Continue until birth of two or more daughters | 95.13 | 82.12 | 88.73 |
| Stop after birth of number of sons | 0.0 | 0.0 | 0.0 |
| No comment | 4.69 | 12.48 | 8.52 |
| **Total** | **100.00** | **100.00** | **100.00** |

**Table 9.5b:** Religion-wise Distribution of Couples According to Values Regarding Additional Child if the First Child is a Son

| *Values regarding additional child if the first child is a son* | *Religion-wise Percentage Distribution of Couples* | | |
|---|---|---|---|
| | *Hindu* | *Niamtre* | *Christian* |
| Continue until birth of one daughter | 0.0 | 0.52 | 0.0 |
| Continue until birth of two or more daughters | 92.42 | 97.40 | 95.73 |
| Stop after birth of number of sons | 0.0 | 0.0 | 0.0 |
| No comment | 7.58 | 2.08 | 4.27 |
| **Total** | **100.00** | **100.00** | **100.00** |

(iv) To support in cultivation or other household works, and

(v) Old age security.

The strong desire to have a daughter is one of the important determinants of high fertility among the Jaintias.

***Acknowledgements***

The author is indebted to her guide, Dr. Bapukan Choudhury, Professor, Department of Anthropology, Gauhati University, Guwahati, for his constant encouragement and valuable suggestions in writing this paper.

**REFERENCES**

Agarwala, S.N. (1972), *India's Population Problems;* Tata McGraw-Hill Publishing Co. Ltd, Bombay-New Delhi.

Bharati, Premananda and Madhusree Ghosh Dastider (1990), "Maternal Education, Fertility and Mortality in a Bengali Population Sample"; *Journal of Indian Anthropological Society;* Vol. 25, pp. 90-93.

Bhende, A. and Tara Kanitkar (1988), *Principals of Population Studies;* Himalayan Publishing House, Bombay; Fourth edition.

Caldwell, J.C. and P. McDonald (1981), "Influence of maternal education on infant and child mortality, levels and causes", International Population Conference, proceedings and selected papers, Manila, 1981; Liege: IUSSP, 2:79-95.

Driver, E.D. (1963), *Differential Fertility in Central India;* Princeton University Press.

Gulati, S.C. (1988), *Fertility in India—An Econometric Analysis of a Metropolis;* Sage Publications, New Delhi.

Hari, M. (1991), "Modernisation, Status of Women and Fertility"; *The Journal of Family Welfare (Personal, Marital and Sociological)* Vol. XXXVII, No. 2, pp. 62-67.

Hussain, I.Z. (1970a), "An urban fertility field: A report on city of Lucknow"; Lucknow: Demographic Research Centre.

Hussain, I.Z. (1970b), "Educational Status and Differential Fertility in India"; *Social Biology*, 17: 132-139.

Krishnan, P. (1986), "Interrelation between fertility and non-economic characteristics", In K. Mahadevan, *et al.* (Ed), *Fertility and Mortality—Theory, Methodology and Empirical Issues*, Sage Publications, pp. 123-135.

Mahadevan, K. and M. Sumangala (1987), Social Development, Cultural Change and Fertility Decline—A Study of Fertility Change in Kerala, Sage Publications, New Delhi.

Nayar, P.K.B. (1986), "Factors in fertility decline in Kerala", In *Fertility and Mortality (Theory Methodology and Empirical Issues)* (eds.) K. Mahadevan with P.J. Reddy and D.A. Naidu, Sage Publications, New Delhi, pp. 155-167.

Thompson Warren and Evangelyn D. Minnis (1953), *Population Problems;* Fourth edition, McGraw-Hill Book Company; INC, New York, Toronto, London, 1953.

UN (1961), "The Mysore Population Study: Report of a field survey carried-out in selected areas of Mysore state, India" pp. 88-226.

Weller, R.H. (1969), "Role conflict and fertility", *Social and Economic Studies*, Jamaica, 18 (3), 263-272 (1969)

# 10

# Understanding the Issue of Child Rights Abuse Arising Due to Physical and Psychological Punishment in Rapar Taluka, Kutch District (Gujarat)

*Chandragupt Sanon* and *Dhanji B. Patel*

## Introduction

Corporal and psychological punishment to children has been a universal phenomenon since time immemorial. It has been a major concern in a civil society comprising of teachers, parents, families, communities and lawmakers in all parts of the world. Controversies continue regarding the adverse effects of corporal and psychological punishment on children—both in school and home (Holden *et al.*, 1991; Hymen *et al.*1966).

Research studies have demonstrated an association between degree/type of punishment and outcome of negative behaviour. However, most studies have originated and have been carried-out in the West. These studies have followed cross-sectional and corelational research design, thereby precluding causal inferences.

Recent studies have begun to examine more closely the influences of culture on perception and interpretation of punishment and its subsequent effects on the child's behaviour. A wide variety of desirable and undesirable behaviour and associated rewards and punishments are taught to the children, both at home and school in various cultures. The perceived cultural meaning of punishment must be carefully examined while conducting any study related to punishment of children.

Another aspect that must be taken into consideration is the possible effect of any form of punishment—physical, social or psychological on the children of various age groups (Cheng, 2000).

**Study Design**

The study design envisaged a participatory research appraisal and employed both qualitative and quantitative methods. The four groups of respondents from whom data were collected are: Adults (parents) and Teachers (through survey questionnaire); Village Elders (through Focus Group Discussion) and Children (through Focus Group Discussion and Participatory Research Appraisal). The study was carried out in two phases between March 31-April 6, 2005 and April 9-15, 2005.

**Profile of Parents**

Nearly two-third parents belonged to the younger age group of below 35 years, in which 71 per cent were Hindu and rest Muslim. Also, nearly half belonged to the Other Backward Class (OBC), while the rest belonged to the category of Scheduled Castes, Scheduled Tribes or General Caste. Literacy level was below national average as over half were illiterate. Out of 48.0 per cent literate, 21.5 per cent had studied only upto class V. As much as 46.5 per cent parents reported agriculture (including agricultural labour and animal husbandry) as their occupation. Those involved in skilled/unskilled labour, business and service sector were smaller in number. Over two-third (67%) lived in nuclear family and the average family size was seven.

**Profile of Teachers**

Majority of the teachers were in the younger age group of 21-35 years. Gender-wise, 51.6 per cent teachers were male and rest female. All teachers were Hindu, in which nearly half belonged to the General Caste and the rest were from Other

Backward Class (32.3%), SC or ST. Over three-fourth teachers were married and lived with their spouses and the remaining 19.4 per cent were unmarried. Majority (51.5%) teachers had either Senior Secondary Certificate or Higher Secondary Certificate, while the rest were graduates or post-graduates. All teachers had either a diploma or degree in education. Over 64.5 per cent teachers were working in Government Schools and among them 70.9 per cent had teaching experience between 1 to 5 years and above.

**Profile of Children**

Six out of ten (60.8%) were boys and the remaining were girls, in which 75 per cent were Hindu and 25 per cent were Muslim. Among Hindus, over half belonged to General Caste, 34.3 per cent to Other Backward Class, and the rest to Scheduled Castes and Scheduled Tribes, thereby indicating larger participation of higher castes in education. Children reported agriculture as the main occupation of their parents, followed by skilled/unskilled labour, business and service. Currently, 73 per cent children were school going, while 14 per cent were dropouts and 11 per cent had never been to school, thereby showing higher participation of children in education.

**Parents' Perception of Discipline and Punishment**

Children performed gender-differentiated roles in varying degrees, though boys were assigned outdoor jobs like bringing provisions from the market, whereas girls were asked to carry out domestic activity like fetching water. Household chores affected studies of children according to 77.0 per cent fathers and 64 per cent mothers. In some villages, children also helped their parents during the harvest season.

In spite of apathy towards educating children, education seemed to have a high priority, as eight out of ten parents said that both boys and girls should be educated which is a positive sign as far as parents' opinion on education is concerned. The real expectation from educating children was that they would improve family income. Therefore, it was considered unnecessary for girls to be educated as much as boys, who were expected to earn a living.

**Necessity of Punishment**

Both father and mother believed that punishment was necessary to discipline the child, particularly to maintain discipline in the family (73.8%). As much as 85 per cent also used fear as a means to discipline children. Fear is created by threatening to report to an elder family member, or call the police or ghost, devil or *sadhu* (saint).

Boys are punished much more than girls for disobeying elders. Male members of the family feel that it is against cultural values for girls to talk too much and too loudly, for which they are punished. It is for this reason that fathers punished daughters (17.8%) more than mothers (5%).

Scolding is the most universal form of punishment, followed by slapping. The focus group discussion with village elders further revealed that the type of punishment depended on the seriousness of the misbehaviour or mistake committed by the children. The most common mode of punishing children is hitting with stick and scolding. There is almost no difference in the way fathers and mothers punished the children. Crying is the most spontaneous response of children to punishment as mentioned by 87 per cent parents. Punishment of any kind meant that the girls start crying immediately.

On the issue of gender-linked punishment to boys and girls, over a third parent's feel that girls and boys should be punished differently; while an equal number are unable to decide. Focus group discussions revealed that at home, girls are generally punished by the mothers whereas boys are punished by both. Boys are considered physically stronger whereas girls are thought to be weaker and milder. Girls are punished less because they are considered *Kawasi* (who will be married into another family) or an incarnation of the goddess.

**Effects of Punishment**

Eight out of ten parents believed that punishment had both positive and negative effects on the children. More than three-fourth parents had noticed improvement in the child's behaviour after punishment. The positive effects are that children begin to obey their parents; girls help mothers with household chores, while negative effects are that children become stubborn. Though three-fourth of the parents punish their children, they also believe there are alternate ways of disciplining children, namely guiding and counselling. Almost all parents found that corporal punishment resulted in pain, violent behaviour and children became reluctant to communicate, often avoiding eye contact.

**Parents' Experience of Punishment during Childhood**

'Disobedience towards the elders' was the most frequent reason for punishment. One-third of the parents have ranked mother as the one who punished children the most. Scolding was the most prevalent form of punishment followed by hitting with stick. Four out of five parents had not experienced any severe punishment in their childhood. However, focus group discussions revealed a different story wherein they were beaten mercilessly with sticks at times after being tied to a tree. Nevertheless, such cases were very few and sporadic. During the present times parents do not punish their children as mercilessly as their parents used to do.

**Awareness of Child Rights**

It is disheartening to know that nearly six out of ten parents were unaware of the rights of the child. Only two out of ten knew about the Child Rights to participate in different types of activities at home and school, right to use leisure time and the right to development. Most parents considered a good diet of vital importance for physical growth of the child. More than half mentioned that good education is important for emotional and intellectual development of the children.

**Children's Participation in Decision-Making**

Nearly two-third parents did not encourage their children to be part of the decision-making process at home and in economic activities. They disagreed that non-participation deprives children of physical or psychological growth. Yet, more than half said that helping out in household chores did deprive children of their right to education and recreation.

**Teachers' Perception of Punishment and Discipline**

***Profile***: Over four-fifth teachers were of the view that they were self-inspired to become teachers. Over half taught languages, social studies/environment, education and mathematics. Teachers often faced problems like lack of cooperation from parents, rampant absenteeism and lack of cooperation from Head Master/Principal. In spite of all these difficulties, 96.9 per cent teachers were satisfied with their work and 74.2 per cent were of the view that quality of education had improved in the last few years.

***Qualities of a Teacher***: Good decision-making skills, regularity in taking classes and the ability to make children understand their lessons were considered important qualities in a teacher. Those who used teaching aids, remain friendly with children, and had the capacity to positively influence children's behaviour were also considered good.

***Reasons for Students' Misbehaviour***: Misbehaviour, according to 54.4 per cent teachers, include not paying attention in class, teasing other children, bullying and threatening classmates. The reasons for such misbehaviour are home environment and poor economic condition. Teachers tried to make children understand their mistakes affectionately and guide and counsel them. In other cases, children were threatened that incidents of misbehaviour would be reported to parents and to the principal. Over half the teachers did not consider punishment necessary to discipline children. Thirty-one per cent advocated guidance and counselling, while the rest felt that punishment was necessary for children to complete school assignments, to maintain discipline in the family and teaching children to respect elders and teachers.

***Fear and Reasons for Punishment***: Over half of the teachers believed in creating fear among children for disciplining them. Teachers punished boys for stealing, quarrelling with classmates, eve teasing and disobedience. However, only 29 per cent teachers punished girls for disobedience, stealing, evading responsibilities and abusing/ quarrelling with classmates.

***Means of Punishment and Reaction*:** Teachers punished children by scolding, making them stand in/outside the classroom, kneel down, temporarily withdrawing benefits, slapping, beating with stick/caning, pinching, assigning extra home work, and making them clean the classroom. Both boys and girls react differently and negatively after being punished in a variety of ways. Important among them were—stopping to talk to each other, complaining about teachers to parents, showing nervousness, tension, restlessness and evading responsibilities. Also, more than one-third of the teachers believed in gender linked punishment, since both boys and girls react differently to punishment. As much as 29 per cent teachers could not express any views about gender-linked punishment.

***Effects of Punishment*:** An overwhelming number of teachers felt that punishment adversely affects children's behaviour but had noticed immediate improvement in the children's behaviour after punishment. Four out of five teachers did not feel that there were alternative ways of disciplining children. Nearly three-fourth teachers saw no negative effects of punishment. Forty-five per cent said punishment causes pain and frightens children. Nine out of ten thought it was wrong to humiliate children in the name of discipline. Almost two-third teachers also believed that punishment affects children's scholastic performance, while four out of ten teachers believed that punishment leads to increase dropout and absenteeism. Enhanced hatred, aggressiveness and violence after punishment were some of the psychological reactions observed by 18.2 per cent teachers.

***Awareness of Child Rights*:** Over eight out of ten teachers were aware of child rights—particularly right to education (52%), right to development (32%), and right to play (28%). Teachers agreed that children should be encouraged to participate in various school activities like games, recreation, fun fair and cultural programmes.

Nearly half teachers admitted that involvement of children in household chores negatively affected their studies/ play. It obstructed their development, and could make them physically weak, and deprived the child of his/her rights. Teachers also gave importance to good diet, physical exercise, space to play, education and a happy family atmosphere for children's physical and emotional growth.

**Children's Perception of Punishment and Discipline**

On the whole, children in the age group 4-6 years believed that it was correct to be punished for not obeying parents. Parents usually punished them by slapping, beating, pinching and scolding. Children's reaction to punishment was by skipping meals, getting angry and crying. Though they resolved to become obedient after punishment yet some of them felt that instead of punishment, they would rather be made to understand their mistakes. Children in the age group of 7-10 years, 11-14 years and 15-18 years expressed similar views.

In the community setting, children (age group 4-6 years) admitted to have done mischievous activities like damaging community property and disobeying elders. Majority requested that they should be helped to understand and explained the negative outcome of such mischief. Children in the age groups 7-10 and 11-14 years had been punished for damaging property and working against the norms and values of the community; whereas children in the 15-18 years age group mentioned that they were scolded for such behaviour.

Children showed improvement after punishment by obeying and doing the assigned work, though they become quiet and reserved for a few days in class. In general, girls are comparatively less punished than boys in all age groups. Girls felt more hurt after being punished than boys in most situations. Older children expressed the view that punishment makes them lose interest in studies, and leads to absenteeism from school and delinquency.

Focus group discussion with children of all standards revealed that irregularity in attending school was a common phenomenon. They liked teachers who taught well, solved their problems and took interest in their studies. They disliked those teachers who punished without reason, humiliated them and did not teach well.

Punishment had both positive and negative effects on children. Positive effects of punishment were that children become regular in studies and negative repercussion was that they become stubborn, obstinate and did not complete homework on time. The types of punishment meted out to older children varies from issuing warnings, sending them back home, calling on parents, making children sweep floors or clean rooms, lobby and compound. In case a student insulted, abused or sometimes showed impertinent behaviour towards teachers, they were even expelled from the school.

Analysis indicated that children had accepted and rationalised punishment by saying that it was for their own good. At the same time, they expressed a strong desire to put their viewpoint across and the need to be understood as individuals. Counselling of children was suggested to help mend their ways. Further, more sensitive treatment of children was suggested.

**Recommendations**

- Punishment to children is being practised in Rapar *taluka* and elsewhere in Gujarat. It has serious repercussions on the physical and psychological well-being of the children. Reduction of punishment is suggested with the help of non-government and government organisations through interactive sessions at least once a month or at a time convenient to the parents, teachers and community elders. It will help them understand the ill effects of corporal punishment and recommend ways to reduce and ultimately eliminate it.
- It is suggested that corporal punishment be applied with great care since it could cause long lasting damages on the self-esteem of the children. All efforts should be made to minimise any type of corporal punishment, whether at home, school or in the

community. Teachers are aware of child's rights, though parents and community elders are relatively less aware. Teachers, but not parents, are also desirous of giving these rights to children, though little is being done to achieve it. Hence, it is recommended that teachers, parents and community leaders must be made aware of the child's rights as a national policy and encouraged to practise it.

- The study has revealed that though the corporal punishment may bring temporary improvement in the behaviour of the children, in the long run, punishment could be counter productive. Therefore, instead of inflicting corporal punishment, the stakeholders should make efforts to help teachers through student meetings to understand each other's expectation in the right perspective. This will help children grow into healthy personalities.
- The study revealed that majority of parents are interested in educating their children, but due to economic compulsions, the children remain absent from school to help their parents. Parents' participation in schemes like *Svarna Jayanti Rojgar Yojana* and Self-Help Groups may ensure that children regularly attend school up to the age of 14 years.
- Irregularities, negligence and certain questionable habits of the teachers have created a poor image of teachers. Hence, strict measures should be enforced by the government, village panchayat and parents to inculcate a sense of social responsibility for good conduct among teachers, particularly in rural areas, where teachers have a vital role in the all-round development of children.
- Teachers should pay special attention in providing positive emotional support to children, understand their problems, avoid psychological maltreatment and harsh forms of corporal punishment. Such an approach would go a long way in creating a positive attitude about studies among children.

Parent-teacher association should be given greater social responsibility for the educational advancement of the children. Radical changes need to be made in the functioning of the village education committees and parent-teacher association wherever they exist. Also, the representatives of the voluntary organisations should work as a 'watch dog' in these committees for bringing improvement in the behaviour of stakeholders and quality of education.

## REFERENCES

Cheng, Karen, O. (2000), *Review of the Literature Regarding the Short and Long Term Consequences of Corporal Punishment on Children*. www.eric.edu (ED 442568).

Holden George. W. *et al.* (1991) *Passing the Rod, Similarities Between Parents and Children's Orientation Towards Physical Punishment*. Research Report, U. S. Texas.

Hymen, Irwin A. *et al.* (1996), *The Enemy Within—Tales of Punishment, Politics and Prevention*. Philadelphia Temple University (National Centre for the Study of Corporal Punishment and Alternatives in the Schools).

*SECTION FOUR*

# Tribal Health, Beliefs and Behavioural Pattern

# 11

# Role of Magico-Religious Healers in Community Health

## A Study of the Tribal Communities of Chhattisgarh

*Narendra Singh* and *Binod C. Agrawal*

### Introduction

In spite of early understanding of diverse human behaviour and social structures in the cultural context of India, anthropological research in health and illness, especially of the Scheduled Tribes, is very limited and scanty. The descriptive analysis of health aspects of Indian Scheduled Tribes and other communities "....have been tentative explorations, with few opportunities of communication and exchange of ideas among interested scholars..." (Scotch, 1963: 33). Medical Anthropology as a sub-field of anthropology has attracted the attention of both modern medical practitioners and anthropologists. Ackerknecht (1942, 1946, 1947: 44-45), the pioneer scholar in medical anthropology wrote "Disease and its treatment are only in the abstract purely biological process. Actually, such facts as whether a person gets sick at all, what kind of disease he acquires and what kind of treatment he receives depended largely upon social factors".

Almost all Scheduled Tribes in India have their own age-old methods of treatment of illnesses, which are based on religion, ritual, sacrifices and medicinal herbs. These Scheduled Tribes believe, like other urban and rural people, in the efficiency of ritual, sacrifice and magic. They believe that such acts can neutralize the effects of "sorcery" with the help of the religious power and can cure the diseases with the help of religious ritual and herbal medicines (Naharia and Vaishnav, 1997). Oudhia (2002) has reported about traditional healers' methods of the treatment and healing practices in the tribal districts of Bastar. The study of traditional healers assumes great significance in India, especially in tribal dominated States, where there seems to be a significant knowledge and understanding gap between the health providers and health seekers, especially among the Scheduled Tribes population. Hence, understanding of the role and function of the traditional healers is essential in order to develop communication health strategy for the implementation of culturally acceptable State Health Services.

Among many academic disciplines, anthropology has contributed a great deal in communication research. Agrawal and his associates carried out formative researches as early as 1974 for providing inputs to Satellite Instructional Television Experiment (SITE) meant for the health and educational development of Chhattisgarh (Agrawal, 2004: 49-55 and Agrawal, 1992: 28-34). Figure 11.1 provides the schematic framework of the formative research for health communication.

At present, scanty information exists about the health communication process in Chhattisgarh where there are 37 per cent Scheduled Tribes and 39 per cent Other Backward Castes (OBCs). They live in rural areas and are mostly dependent on magico-religious healers for healthcare. It is therefore imperative to involve magico-religious healers in improving the effective utilization of State Health Services. The present formative research is expected to provide research inputs for evolving health communication strategy for the State of Chhattisgarh.

**Study Area**

The study was conducted in four districts of Chhattisgarh, namely Bastar, Dantewada, Jaspur and Sarguja. The State of

Chhattisgarh came into existence in November 2000 as the 26th State of the Indian Republic. According to 2001 census, the State has sixteen districts with 192,000 sq. km. area and over 275 million populations. The sex ratio of the State is 990 females per 1000 males—one of the few States having an almost equal sex ratio. The literacy rate of the State is 65 per cent. Scheduled Tribes population of the State is 37 per cent, 39 per cent are Other Backward Castes and 15 per cent of the population are Scheduled Castes. The rural populace is predominantly tribal in its demography and the State is home to 42 different tribes. Agriculture is the mainstay for more than 80 per cent of the people in spite of rich natural resources. The major Tribes of the State are Oraon, Gond, Nagwanshi, Kowar, Kumhar, Koyta, Korwa, Halba, Panka, Gada, Satnami, Konda, Valar, Bhatra, Marar, Mahbu.

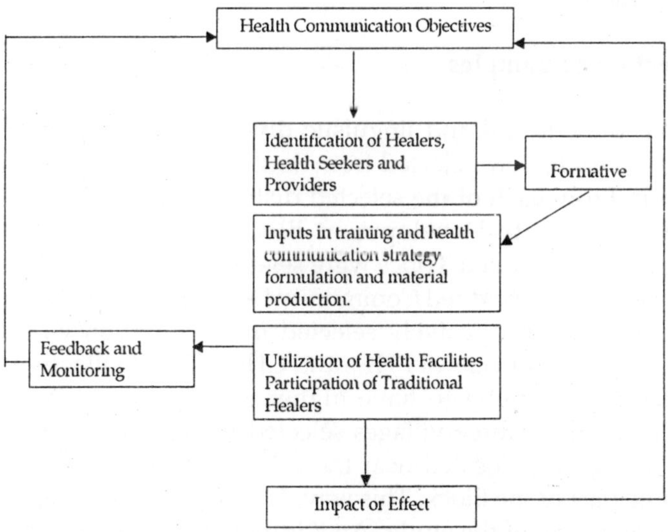


**Fig. 11.1:** Conceptual Framework for the Health Communication

## Objectives

Keeping in mind the unique cultural characteristics of the State, an attempt has been made to carryout such a study among the magico-religious healers.

1. To understand and identify the role of healers towards community health.
2. To findout how healers perceive and contribute towards the modern health system.

## Research Design

In light of the objectives and taking into account the nature of the study, it is proposed to follow an ethnographic holistic approach for the collection of qualitative, descriptive and in-depth data. It would involve in-depth interviews and participant observations. Given the time constraint classical anthropological methods and techniques of long duration fieldwork was not possible. Information was gathered by using open-ended interview schedule, focus group interviews and case study.

## Selection of Samples

Given the cultural and linguistic diversity of the State, two districts each were selected from Southern and North-eastern region. From each of the selected districts of the two regions, one Community Development Block having numerically dominant Scheduled Tribes were selected.

From each selected Community Development Block, three villages were purposively selected in consultation with the Block Health Officials of PHCs and CHCs. These villages were selected presuming to have higher numbers of traditional healers. Out of three villages selected in each Block, at least one village was located near the urban centre and other in a remote part of the Block. This way, 12 villages were covered in the first phase of the study. An additional remote village was covered from Pathalgaon Block of Jashpur District in the second phase of the Study as recommended in the review workshop held on February 1, 2005. Thus in all, 13 villages were covered (Table 11.1). A total of 50 magico-religious healers were covered in the present study.

All these villages have hand pumps as a source of drinking water. The educational facilities include primary schools in every sample village and a few of them also have middle schools. Except few, most of them do not have post office or health centre. The traditional healers are prevalent in every village, so are various means of communications, though there are great deals of variations among the villages.

**Table 11.1:** Distribution of Selected Samples by Village, Block and District

| *District* | *Block* | *Village* | *Sample* |
|---|---|---|---|
| Sarguja | Sitapur | 1. Sarga | 03 |
| | | 2. Bhithua | 05 |
| | | 3. Dhelsara | 04 |
| Jashpur | Pathalgaon | 4. Kachchar | 04 |
| | | 5. Shekharpur | 03 |
| | | 6. Sukhrapara | 04 |
| | | 7. Balajhar | 04 |
| Dantewada | Geedam | 8. Madse | 05 |
| | | 9. Ronje | 04 |
| | | 10. Pharspad | 04 |
| Bastar | Kondagaon | 11. Bade Kanera | 03 |
| | | 12. Chimdi | 03 |
| | | 13. Bafna | 04 |

## Findings

A magico-religious healer is a person who is consulted to heal or treat a patient using spiritual power, religious power, magical power or with a combination of all. The treatment by an indigenous *healer* of illnesses considered to be brought about by such influences is known as *magico-religious* treatment. There are two approaches as to who can become a magico-religious healer (i) One can learnt either from his parents or family members (ancestral); (ii) After the possession of spirit by a person, *devi* comes in the dream of the person and asked to join in the profession.

**Magico-religious healers** are known by different names in the State such as *Baiga, Gunia, Sirha, Deowar* and *Vaid.*

There are three categories of traditional healers based on the mode of treatment: Religious, herbal and religio-herbal. The prevalence of religious methods to treat illnesses is overwhelming.

1. *Herbal Healers*: *Vaidya, Baiga, Gunia* and *Deowar*, who treat patients suffering from bodily illnesses and exclusively by herbal medicines.
2. *Religious Healers*: *Sirha*, who treats the sick persons inflicted or possessed by benign or malign spirits, or supernatural powers like *bhoot-pret* (ghost and evil spirits), evil eye and/or due to disobedience of *devi-devta* (Gods and Goddesses).
3. *Religio-herbal Healer*: *Baiga, Gunia* and *Deowar* perform both rituals and sacrifices for diagnosis and administer herbal medicines for treatment. Almost everyone except *Sirha* falls in this category.

**Socio-economic Background**

Almost all healers are male, with the exception of one female from Sarguja district, indicating that traditional healing is a male-dominated activity. With regard to age, over three-fourth of them belong to age 31-60 age group. A healer needs years of experience to gain expertise. Regardless of literacy and education levels, healers are almost uniformly poor. Nearly two-third falls in the household income category of less than Rs. 500 to Rs. 1000 a month. In other words, healers belong to the poor strata of the community. The average household size of the healers is 5.5 members and most of them live in *Kachcha* houses.

**Professional Background**

More than half of the healers have been treating and healing patents for more than 16 years. Traditional healing runs in the family, as healers acknowledge the existence of other healers in the family. For most of them, it is "part time" or "only when required". Healing is not the main source of income; most of them have some other primary occupation as a means of livelihood. The healers have a genuine concern and social obligation towards the health of the community. Neither healer nor community members expressed "earning money" as a motivation for healers to remain in the profession. Three factors that were rated as 'important' for a healer were: literacy, determination and a willingness to learn the art of healing.

**Role of Healers**

Exception apart, uniformly, the community at large knows the existence and usefulness of healers. So the existence of healers and their positive role for providing health care is beyond question.

Consultation through face-to-face communication is reported by a large number of individuals interviewed in the study. Accessibility to healers is undeniable and the same was repeatedly reaffirmed during various discussions and supplemented through observations. A healer can be approached for consultation, diagnosis and treatment at any time of the day or night. In case of non-availability, another healer can be approached to provide similar service, or the patient waits until the healer is available. Not a single respondent had indicated refusal of any kind by the healers at any time. The operative method of seeking treatment is to go to the healer's place of stay alone or accompanied by family members.

Access and approach to more than one healer is an independent family or patient's decision. The advice of the healer is generally followed by the patients and their family members.

Given the linguistic and dialectical diversity of Chhattisgarh, exchange of health information for the purpose of diagnosis and treatment, sharing common linguistic code is very important between the healer, patient and family members. Since the patient and their family members approach the local healers in most cases, they exchange and share health information without distortion. Even when patients are referred to healers of other villages, the patient remained within the linguistice and dialectical boundary, so no information is lost in the discourse. Local name of diseases, experiences of pain, fever, parts of the body, are verbalized and understood, which helps the diagnosis and subsequent prescription of the line of treatment—whether religious, herbal or religio-herbal.

**Credibility of the Healer**

Credibility of the traditional healer is observed to be extremely high all across the community. Even some of the doctors and other health-workers recognize the importance of the healers and consider them highly credible and respect them for their healing knowledge and skills. Even the educated sceptics recognize the considerable prestige the healers enjoy. Almost all the informants, during individual interviews have indicated direct *face-to-face* interaction with at least one of the healers and having been treated by them. Also some of them accept that they have been fully or partially cured by the healers.

By and large, a healer is approached first in nearly 90 per cent of the cases. However, 10 per cent of them have indicated not going to a healer for treatment.

Everyone has unanimously agreed that the cost of healers' treatment is much cheaper, not requiring cash or immediate expenditure and that the healers make no demands to the patient or family. The important point is that there is a single window treatment and expenditure of healers is affordable, that too without running around. Whereas in case of doctors, it has multiple steps like from doctor to the technician, X-ray, pathologist or pharmacist and so on.

**Healers Contribution to Community**

Healers claim that people of all strata of society consult them—the literate, illiterate, the poor and the well to do. The healers are consulted for any kind of sickness/illness in the community. They further mentioned that service to community and people's faith in them motivates them to continue in this profession. Exception apart, the community at large acknowledges the usefulness of healers. They are accessible at any time of the day and night; and in case of serious illnesses, are willing to go to the patient.

The healers share a common linguistic code with the community that he serves, ensuring that there is no distortion in the exchange of information between healer and patient, given the variety of dialects that are spoken in Chhattisgarh. This way they have an edge over the medical doctors of the State Health Services, with whom the patients often experience a communication gap. Besides, healers are accountable and recommend a follow-up visit when necessary. In many cases the healer is unsuccessful; he refers the patient to another healer or a doctor.

A sense of service to the community and people's faith in the healer's skill motivate healers in continuing to practice healing. They show a genuine concern towards the health and well-being of the community. They do not hesitate to visit the patient if so required, and expect no immediate gift or cash in return.

**Recommendations**

(a) Healers may be trained to provide information to the community members regarding modern health care services available in the health centres. Also, there is a need to communicate with the community members regarding importance and effectiveness of modern medicine.
(b) Since healers and community members share a common linguistic code, exchange of health information is more meaningful. Hence, a catalyst between modern health system and community. Healers can be assigned responsibility for providing health messages to their own hamlets.
(c) Health awareness campaign must be organized regularly at the village level in which healers may be given responsibility to encourage community's participation.

**REFERENCES**

Ackerknecht, E.H. (1942), Problems of Primitive Medicine. *Bull. Hist. Med.* 11: 503-21.

Adair, J.K., Deuschle and W. McDermott (1957), Patterns of Health and Diseases Among the Navahos, *Ann. Amer. Acad. Pol. Soc. Sci.* 311: 80-94.

Agrawal, Binod C. (1985), *Anthropological Methods for Communication Research.* Concept Publishing Company, New Delhi.

Jha, N. and A.T. Kannan (1999), Utilizing Traditional Healers in Primary Health Care; *Regional Health Forum;* Vol. 5, No. 2.

Mibang, T. and S.K. Choudhury (eds.) (2003), *Ethnomedicine of the Tribes of Arunachal Pradesh,* Itanagar: Himalayan Publisher.

Nharia, A.L. and T.K.K. Vaishnav (1997), Indegenous Knowledge of Ethno (Herbal) Medicine among Tribes of Patalkot Valley—MP: *Bulletin of the Tribal Research Institute,* Bhopal, Vol. XXV, No. 2 pp. 30-31 .

Scotch, N.A. (1963), Medical Anthropology. In *Biennial Review of Anthropology,* (ed.) Bernard J. Siegel, p. 54, Stanford University Press, Stanford, California.

# Index